MAKING RADICAL DISCIPLES

A manual to facilitate training
disciples in house churches,
small groups, and discipleship
groups, leading towards a
church-planting movement.

Making Radical Disciples

A training manual to facilitate training disciples in house churches, small groups, and discipleship groups, leading towards a church-planting movement.

By Daniel B. Lancaster, Ph.D.

Published by:

T4T Press

First Printing, 2011

ISBN978-0-9831387-0-9 printed

Library of Congress Cataloging-in-Publication Data

Lancaster, Daniel B.
Making Radical Disciples: A training manual to facilitate training disciples in house churches, small groups, and discipleship groups, leading towards a church-planting movement. / Daniel B. Lancaster.
Includes bibliographical references.
ISBN 978-0-9831387-0-9
1. Follow Jesus Training: Basic Discipleship–United States.
I. Title.

Recommendations

"There is always a need for books which see mission expansion and church growth through the eyes of experience and dedication. Follow Jesus Training is such a series. It simplifies the strategy of Jesus to reach the nations of today's world.

This book is written by a practitioner, not merely a theoretician. You will be richer from having read and studied Follow Jesus Training, a fresh approach from the pen of veteran missionary Dan Lancaster."

Roy J. Fish
Professor Emmeritus
Southwestern Baptist Theological Seminary

"Looking for something practical to make disciples of seekers and new believers in any culture group? This is it!

A three-day, discipleship-training manual that is so easy to follow that new disciples can use it to train others, in turn, for instant, loving obedience to the commands of Jesus. Dan Lancaster has taken tons of experience, best practices and Scripture, and put them into a tool that I will be carrying with me."

Galen Currah
Paul Timothy Trainers Itinerant Consultant
www.Paul-Timothy.net

"The clear and repetitive approach of these discipleship materials provides an effective framework for the new believer understanding and mastering the basics of the faith, and sharing with others that which he or she is learning."

Clyde D. Meador
Executive Vice President
International Mission Board, SBC

"I have taught this material to 100s of leaders here in America and I always get the same two replies, 'This is so simple' and 'I wish I had been taught this years ago.' The truth in this manual is viral, practical, proven, and effective in making disciples who make disciples. I recommend it wholeheartedly!"

Roy McClung
Missionary/Consultant
www.MaximizeMyMinistry.com

"This is a catechism for the CPM world. It is a simple application of a scalable process to provide a basic framework for a fruitful life of discipleship. It is filled with valuable, practical training tips."

Curtis Sergeant
Vice President for Global Strategies
E3 Partners Ministry
www.e3partners.org

"Following Jesus Training Book One–Making Radical Disciples is the kind of practical discipleship tool that new believers around the world can use to establish their foundation in Jesus. It teaches believers to love God with all their heart, soul, mind and strength. It also provides tools that new believers as well as more mature believers can use as they communicate the love of Christ.

From day one they are taught concern for a lost and dying world. They are taught to share what they have learned as they advance into areas of darkness with the light of Jesus. It is practical, user-friendly, biblical, and bold."

Gerald W. Burch
Missionary Emeritus
International Mission Board, SBC

"Dan Lancaster has provided a simple, biblical, and reproducible method for producing radical follower of Christ. What else are you looking for? Dan uses eight simple pictures of Jesus to help believers grow in the Lord. These principles have been tested in the crucible of mission experience and will work for you."

Ken Hemphill
National Strategist for Empowering Kingdom Growth
Author, Speaker, Growth Consultant, and Professor of Evangelism and Church Growth

"I have used this material in the Philippines and love it because IT WORKS. I asked my trainees why they liked the material and they responded, "Because the ones we teach can train others also!" This is the great value in these simple lessons ... they are REPRODUCIBLE.

We have seen lawyers, doctors, Army colonels, businessmen, widows, and guards at the gate, the educated and the uneducated all use this material to train others who are training even others."

Darrel Seale
Missionary in the Philippines

"As a career church planter in both rural and urban areas of Thailand for over 30 years, too often I saw "atrophied churches"–ones which continued to depend on outside leaders for most of their spiritual nourishment. This condition was caused largely because those who planted those churches used western-oriented teaching methods which were not reproducible by the national believers. Few of those churches ever reproduced themselves–they were crippled from birth!

This training manual gives us two keys to assure that the Word will be passed on from believer to believer: the simplicity of reproducibility and repetition."

Jack Kinnison
Missionary Emeritus
International Mission Board, SBC

"Jesus said that if anyone wanted to be his disciple, he must 'deny himself and take up his cross and follow him.' As a teacher, pastor, father and missionary, Dan Lancaster understands the foundational and irreplaceable demands of discipleship. This training is valuable, strategic and appropriate for the remote village as well as the university classroom.

The call to discipleship is universal and Dr. Lancaster has created a tool usable and reproducible in every culture and setting. Using simple and solid teaching methods, FJT makes discipleship training both fun and memorable. Follow Jesus Training is the entire package for disciples: biblical, reproducible, practical, and multiplying."

Bob Butler
Country Director
Cooperative Services International
Phnom Penh, Kingdom of Cambodia

"Dr. Dan Lancaster has carefully studied not only the Gospels but also culture. He has given us a simple and doable process for helping people grow strong in the Lord that follows the methods of Jesus without becoming 'program oriented'. This process for House Churches is Christ centered and disciple oriented. I highly commend this process and pray it will transcend the House Church culture and also be used in the traditional church in North America."

Ted Elmore
Prayer Strategist and Field Ministry Strategist
Southern Baptists of Texas Convention

Contents

Part 1: Nuts And Bolts

Part 2: Training

Part 3: Reference

Foreword

"...and teach them to observe all things
whatsoever I have commanded you."

These closing words to the Great Commission remain as important and challenging for us today as they were when Christ first issued them 2,000 years ago. What does it mean to observe all things that Christ commanded? The Apostle John tells us that if we were to write down everything Jesus said and did, it would fill all the books of the world (John 21:25). Certainly, Jesus had in mind something more succinct. In part one of Follow Jesus Training, subtitled *Making Radical Disciples,* Dan Lancaster has drawn out of the Gospels eight pictures of Jesus which, when emulated, can transform a follower of Christ into a Christ-like disciple.

In *Making Radical Disciples,* Dan has aimed higher than simply producing another book about discipleship. Dan set his sights on creating a discipleship multiplication movement. To this end, he spent four years crafting, testing, evaluating, and revising his discipleship program until he was seeing it not only transform new believers into Christ-like disciples, but also turning these trained disciples into effective disciple makers themselves.

After developing this discipleship system, Dr. Lancaster has done the entire body of Christ a service by condensing these lessons into a user-friendly, reproducible format that can be adapted to any cultural setting in the world. *Making Radical Disciples* is a dynamic contribution to the never-ending pursuit of being like Jesus and multiplying Christ's kingdom through new disciples throughout the world.

Making disciples in an age steeped in the ways of this world is not easy, but neither is it impossible, nor is it optional. As you dive into Dan Lancaster's *Making Radical Disciples*, you will meet a fellow disciple and disciple maker who can show you a tested and proven roadmap for the way ahead.

David Garrison
Chiang Mai, Thailand

Acknowledgements

Thank you to the members of three churches in America where Follow Jesus Training began fifteen years ago: Community Bible Church, Hamilton, Texas (a rural church plant); New Covenant Baptist Church, Temple, Texas (an established discipleship-focused church); and Highland Fellowship, Lewisville, Texas (a suburban church plant). Over the years, we saw FJT grow from four to seven, and finally eight, pictures of Christ. We shared much together, and your love and prayers have resulted in fruitfulness to the nations!

National partners in several Southeast Asian countries helped refine and implement Follow Jesus Training internationally. Because of security and safety concerns in these countries, I cannot disclose their names. In particular, a group of three nationals helped field-test the training and continue to train succeeding generations of disciples to train others.

Thank you to the many training participants who gave prayerful support, feedback, and encouragement throughout the four-year development process in Southeast Asia. You helped focus and improve the training in significant ways.

Each of us is the product of the investment of mentors and life experiences. I would like to thank Rev. Ronnie Capps, Dr. Roy J. Fish, Craig Garrison, Dr. David Garrison, Dr. Elvin McCann, Rev. Dylan Romo, and Dr. Thom Wolf for the impact they have had on my life as a disciple of Jesus.

Special thanks to Drs. George Patterson and Galen Currah for several of the active learning skits in this training.

Special thanks, as well, to Bonita Hele for editing and formatting this version of the book.

Finally, I thank my family for their support and encouragement. My children, Jeff, Zach, Karis, and Zane, continue to be an unending source of faith, hope, and love.

Holli, my wife, did a remarkable job reading the manuscript many times and offering suggestions. She added several good ideas from the training seminars she has led and has been a faithful sounding board for many of the concepts, hammered out over the last fifteen years.

May God bless you all, as we continue to develop passionate, spiritual leaders and bring healing to the nations!

Daniel B. Lancaster, Ph.D.
January 2011
Southeast Asia

Introduction

Welcome to *Making Radical Disciples*, part one of Follow Jesus Training (FJT)! May God bless and prosper you as you follow his Son. May the fruitfulness of your ministry increase a hundredfold as you walk slowly with Jesus through your "unreached people group" (UPG).

The manual you hold in your hands is a complete training system based on Jesus' strategy to reach the world. It is the result of years of research and testing in both North America and Southeast Asia. This system is not theory, but practice. Use it to make a real difference in the world as you are on your mission with God. We have and you can, too.

After starting a rural church and a suburban church in America, our family sensed a call to Southeast Asia to coach and train leaders. I had been a church planter in America for over ten years and had coached other church planters as well. How hard could it be to move overseas and do the same thing there? Our family left for the mission field with hubris and high hopes.

During language learning, I began to train others with a national partner. We started by offering a one-week training course on basic discipleship and church planting. Typically, thirty to forty students would come to the training. They often commented on how good the lessons were and how much they appreciated our teaching. But one thing began to bother me: it was evident that they were not teaching others what they had learned.

Now in America you can "get away with them not teaching others" because there is (or has been) a biblical understanding at the center of our culture, even among lost people. In Southeast Asia, however, no biblical understanding exists among the lost. In America, you might count on the fact that this person will probably encounter another Christian who will influence them; on the mission field, no such guarantee exists.

OK, so here we were in a quandary. We were teaching the nationals what we felt was "good stuff", but they were not reproducing it. In fact, it seemed like we were attracting "professional seminar goers." The fact that we provided meals at the weeklong training in a country overwhelmed with poverty mired the results, too. What happened next surprised and humbled me.

After one of our training events, I sat down in a teashop with my interpreter and asked him a simple question:

"John. *How much of the training we did this week do you think the folks will actually do and train others to do?"*

John thought about it for a while and I could tell he didn't want to answer me. In his culture, a student never comments on or critiques a teacher and he felt like that was what I was asking him to do. After more conversation and assurances from me, he gave a response that changed everything:

"Dr. Dan, I think they will do about ten percent of what you taught them this past week."

I was stunned and tried not to show it. Instead, I asked John another question that started a process we would follow for the next two and a half years:

"John, can you show me the ten percent you think they will do or are doing? My plan is to keep that ten percent, throw out the rest, and rewrite the training until they do everything we train them to do."

---

* Name changed for security reasons.

16

John showed me the ten percent he believed they would actually do. We discarded the rest and rewrote the training for the next meeting. One month later, we offered another weeklong training and I asked John the same question afterwards: What percent will they do?

John said, "Dr. Dan, I am pretty sure they will do fifteen percent of what you taught this time."

I was speechless. What John didn't know is that I had rewritten the training from the previous month, putting in the "best of the best" of everything I had learned as a pastor in America and while coaching other church planters. That seminar had the best I had to give… and the learners were only going to do fifteen percent of it!

Thus began the process that we used for two and a half years, refining and developing the Follow Jesus Training system. Each month, we taught a one-week seminar and had a feedback session after the seminar was complete. One question guided our efforts: what percent of what we taught them will they do (or are doing) because of the training?

By the third month, our percentage rose to twenty percent; the next month, it went to twenty-five. Some months we made no progress at all. Other months, we leaped ahead. Throughout the development phase, however, one clear principle emerged. The more we trained others to follow Jesus' example, the more likely they were to train others to do the same.

I still remember the day John and other nationals shared with me that the people we had trained were doing ninety percent of what we had taught them to do. We had long since left our western methods, our Asian methods, our PhD training, our experiences, and learned to trust in nothing but the example Jesus left us to follow.

That is the story of how Follow Jesus Training (FJT) came to be. *Making Radical Disciples* is a hands-on training system that equips believers to follow the five steps of Jesus' strategy to reach the nations seen in the Gospels, the book of Acts, the Epistles, and Church history. The goal of the training journey is transformation and not information. For that reason, lessons are simple "seeds" of key spiritual truths; what is more, they are highly reproducible. They follow the spiritual principle, "a little leaven leavens the whole lump" and empower believers to become reproducing, passionate followers of Christ.

A suggestion: teach the material in this manual, step-by-step, five times before you change anything (other than adapting the training to the cultural setting where you work). Let the first five times you facilitate *Making Radical Disciples* be as if the training team is walking beside you, guiding you as you train others. *Making Radical Disciples* has several over-arching dynamics that are not obvious until you have trained others step-by-step several times. To date, we have trained thousands of individuals, believers and unbelievers, with this material in both Southeast Asia and America. Follow this suggestion to avoid mistakes others have already made! Remember: a smart man learns from his mistakes; a wise man learns from the mistakes of others.

As you begin, we must share with you that Follow Jesus Training has changed us as much as it has changed anyone we have trained. May God do the same and abundantly more in your life!

Part 1

Nuts

and

Bolts

Jesus' Strategy

Jesus' strategy to reach the nations involves five steps: grow strong in the Lord, share the gospel, make disciples, start groups that lead to churches, and develop leaders. Each step stands alone, but also amplifies the other steps in a circular process. The material in FJT empowers trainers to be a catalyst for a church-planting movement among their people by following Jesus.

Making Radical Disciples addresses the first three steps: Grow Strong in the Lord, Share the Gospel, and Make Disciples. Learners are given a vision for multiplication and are trained in how to: lead a small group, pray, obey Jesus' commands, and walk in the power of the Holy Spirit (Grow Strong in the Lord). Learners then discover how to join God wherever they might be working; they learn how to share their testimony, sow the gospel, and share a vision with others for multiplication among their people (Share the Gospel). Completing the course gives learners the tools to make disciples (step three) and guide them into groups.

Learners who are faithful to train others using *Making Radical Disciples* may continue with either *Starting Radical Churches* or *Training Radical Leaders,* depending upon their needs. *Starting Radical Churches* is a training system designed to empower churches to start new groups and churches, leading to a church-planting movement (the fourth step in Jesus' strategy). *Training Radical Leaders* is a training system created to develop passionate, spiritual leaders, heading towards the eventual goal of a church-planting movement (the fifth step in Jesus' strategy). Both training systems explore Jesus' ministry and method, giving learners simple, reproducible tools that they can master and share with others.

The following scriptures confirm the five steps mentioned above in the ministry of Jesus. The strategy of Peter and Paul demonstrates that they imitated Jesus by following the same pattern. Follow Jesus Training enables us to do the same.

JESUS

GROW STRONG IN THE LORD

—Luke 2:52—And Jesus increased in wisdom and stature, and in favor with God and men.

22

SHARE THE GOSPEL

—Mark 1:14, 15—Now after John was put in prison, Jesus came to Galilee, preaching the gospel of the kingdom of God, and saying, "The time is fulfilled, and the kingdom of God is at hand. Repent, and believe in the gospel."

MAKE DISCIPLES

—Mark 1:16-18—And as He walked by the Sea of Galilee, He saw Simon and Andrew his brother casting a net into the sea; for they were fishermen. Then Jesus said to them, "Follow Me, and I will make you become fishers of men." They immediately left their nets and followed Him.

START GROUPS/CHURCHES

—Mark 3:14, 15—Then He appointed twelve, that they might be with Him and that He might send them out to preach, and to have power to heal sicknesses and to cast out demons.(See also Mark 3:16-19, 31,35)

TRAIN LEADERS

—Mark 6:7-10—And He called the twelve to Himself, and began to send them out two by two, and gave them power over unclean spirits. He commanded them to take nothing for the journey except a staff—no bag, no bread, no copper in their money belts—but to wear sandals, and not to put on two tunics. Also He said to them, "In whatever place you enter a house, stay there till you depart from that place." (See also Mark 6:11-13)

PETER

GROW STRONG IN THE LORD

—Acts 1:13, 14—When they had come in, they went up into the upper room, where they were staying; that is Peter, John, James.... All these with one accord continued steadfastly in prayer and supplication, along with the women, and Mary the mother of Jesus, and with his brothers.

SHARE THE GOSPEL

—Acts 2:38, 39—Then Peter said to them, "Repent, and let every one of you be baptized in the name of Jesus Christ for the remission of sins; and you shall receive the gift of the Holy Spirit. For the promise is to you and to your children, and to all who are afar off, as many as the Lord our God will call."

MAKE DISCIPLES

—Acts 2:42, 43—And they continued steadfastly in the apostles' doctrine and fellowship, in the breaking of bread, and in prayers. Then fear came upon every soul, and many wonders and signs were done through the apostles.

START GROUPS/CHURCHES

—Acts 2:44-47—Now all who believed were together, and had all things in common, and sold their possessions and goods, and divided them among all, as anyone had need. So

continuing daily with one accord in the temple, and breaking bread from house to house, they ate their food with gladness and simplicity of heart, praising God and having favor with all the people. And the Lord added to the church daily those who were being saved.

TRAIN LEADERS

—Acts 6:3, 4—"Therefore, brethren, seek out from among you seven men of good reputation, full of the Holy Spirit and wisdom, whom we may appoint over this business; but we will give ourselves continually to prayer and to the ministry of the word." (See also Acts 6:5, 6)

PAUL

GROW STRONG IN THE LORD

—Galatians 1:15-17—But when it was the good pleasure of God, who separated me from my mother's womb, and called me through his grace, to reveal his Son in me, that I might preach him among the Gentiles, I didn't immediately confer with flesh and blood, nor did I go up to Jerusalem to those who were apostles before me, but I went away into Arabia. Then I returned to Damascus.

SHARE THE GOSPEL

—Acts 14:21—And when they had preached the gospel to the city of Derbe and made many disciples, they returned to Lystra, Iconium, and Antioch....

MAKE DISCIPLES

> *—Acts 14:22—...strengthening the souls of the disciples, exhorting them to continue in the faith, and saying, "We must through many tribulations enter the kingdom of God."*

START GROUPS/CHURCHES

> *—Acts 14:23—So when they had appointed elders in every church, and prayed with fasting, they commended them to the Lord in whom they had believed.*

TRAIN LEADERS

> *—Acts 16:1—Then he came to Derbe and Lystra. And behold, a certain disciple was there, named Timothy, the son of a certain Jewish woman who believed, but his father was Greek. (See also Acts 16: 2, 3)*

CHURCH HISTORY

Throughout Church history, this same five-step process is clear. Whether St. Benedict, St. Francis of Assisi, Peter Waldo and the Waldensians, Jacob Spener and the Pietists, John Wesley and the Methodists, Jonathan Edwards and the Puritans, Gilbert Tennant and the Baptists, Dawson Trotman and the Navigators, Billy Graham and modern evangelicalism, or Bill Bright and Campus Crusade for Christ, the same pattern emerges over and over again.

Jesus said, *"I will build my church"* in Matthew 16:18. This pattern is his method and FJT empowers believers to follow Jesus with all their heart, soul, mind, and strength.

Training Trainers

This section details how to train trainers in a reproducible way. First, we will share with you the outcomes you can reasonably expect after training others with *Making Radical Disciples*. Then, we will outline for you the process of training, which includes 1) worship, 2) prayer, 3) study, and 4) practice, based on the most important commandment. Finally, we share some of the key principles in training trainers we have discovered while training thousands of trainers.

Outcomes

After finishing *Making Radical Disciples*, learners will be able to:

- Teach ten basic discipleship lessons based on Christ to others, using a reproducible training process.
- Recall eight clear pictures that portray a follower of Jesus.
- Lead a simple, small-group worship experience based on the most important commandment.
- Share a powerful testimony and gospel presentation with confidence.
- Present a concrete vision for reaching the lost and training believers using an Acts 29 Map.
- Start a disciple group (some of which will become churches) and train others to do the same.

Process

Each session follows the same format. Listed below is the order and estimated timetable:

PRAISE

- 10 minutes
- Ask someone to open the session, praying for God's blessing and direction for everyone in the group. Enlist someone in the group to lead a few choruses or hymns (depending on your context); an instrument is optional.

PRAYER

- 10 minutes
- Divide learners into pairs with someone they have not been a partner with before. Partners share with each other the answer to two questions:

  1. How can we pray for lost people you know to be saved?
  2. How can we pray for the group you are training?

- If a learner has not started a group, their partner should work with them to develop a list of possible friends and family to train, then pray with the learner for people on their list.

STUDY

The Follow Jesus Training system uses two tracks during the study section based on the simple worship model. The material below explains the first track, which consists of the ten lessons in this manual. The second track runs concurrent to the first track and is composed of lessons based on Bible stories. Turn to page 23 in the section "Simple Worship" for more details concerning the second track.

- 30 minutes
- Each "Study" section starts with "Review." It is a review of the eight pictures of Christ and lessons mastered thus far. By the end of the training, learners will be able to recite the whole training by memory.
- After "Review," the trainer or apprentice trains learners with the current lesson, emphasizing that learners should listen closely because they will be training each other afterwards.
- When trainers present the lesson, they should use the following sequence:

  1. Ask the question.
  2. Read the Scripture.
  3. Encourage learners to answer the question.

This process places the word of God as authority for life and not the teacher. Too often, teachers ask a question, give the answer, and then support their answer with Scripture. That sequence puts the teacher as the authority, rather than the word of God.

- If learners answer the question incorrectly, do not correct them, but ask participants to read the Scripture passage aloud and answer again.
- Each lesson ends with a memory verse. Trainers and learners stand together and recite the memory verse ten times; saying the verse address first, followed by the verse. Learners may use their Bibles or student guides the first six times they say the memory verse. The last four times, however, the group recites the memory verse from the heart. The entire group recites the verse ten times and then sits down.

PRACTICE

- 30 minutes
- Previously, the trainers divided learners for the "Prayer" segment. Their prayer partner is also their practice partner.
- Each lesson has a method of choosing who the "leader" of the pair will be. The leader is the person who will teach first. The trainer announces the method of choosing the leader of the pair to the group.
- Imitating the trainers, the leader trains their partner. The training period should include the review and the new lesson, and end with the memory verse. Learners stand to recite the "Memory Verse" and sit when it is complete, so trainers can see which learners have finished.
- When the first person in a pair finishes, the second person repeats the process, so they can practice training as well. Ensure that the pair does not skip or take shortcuts in the process.
- Walk around the room while they are practicing to make sure they are following you exactly. Failing to do the hand motions is a dead giveaway that they are not imitating you. Emphasize repeatedly that they should copy you, the trainer.

ENDING

- 20 minutes
- Most sessions end with a practical application learning activity. Give learners plenty of time to work on their Acts 29 Maps and encourage them to walk around and get ideas from others as they work.
- Make any necessary announcements, and then ask someone to pray a blessing on the session. Ask someone who has not prayed before to pray—by the end of the training, everyone should have closed in prayer at least once.

PRINCIPLES

We discovered the following principles in the midst of teaching thousands of people the last ten years. In our experience, the principles are not culturally specific; we have seen them at work in Asia, America, and Africa (we don't know about Europe, yet!).

- *The Rule of Five:* Learners must practice a lesson five times before they have the confidence necessary to train another person. Practicing a lesson includes either "seeing" or "doing." For that reason, we recommend doing the practice time twice. Learners should practice once with their prayer partner and then switch to another partner and do the lesson again.

- *Less Is Better Than More:* Most learners are educated far above their obedience level. A common mistake among trainers is giving their learners far more information than they can obey. Long-term exposure to this type of training leaves learners full of knowledge with little practical application. We always try to give the learner a "backpack" of information that they can carry with them and apply, not a "crate."

- *Different Learners Learn Differently:* People approach learning from three different styles: auditory, visual, and kinesthetic. For training to be highly reproducible, it must involve all three styles of learning in each lesson. Most training, however, relies on one or two styles at the most. Our goal is to see transformation across an entire group of people. Our training system, as a result, incorporates all three learning styles in order to exclude no one.

- *Process and Content are Important:* Researchers have discovered many advances in adult education that empower us to teach people in a transformational, rather than informational, way. For example, we know that the "lecture format" often used is not a good methodology of

31

learning for the majority of students. Sadly, most training done overseas still follows this pattern. We concentrate on reproducibility in the Follow Jesus Training system—evaluating our lessons on the ability of the next generation of learners to reproduce them.

- *Review, Review, Review:* Another term often used for memorizing is "learning something by heart." Our training system is all about seeing people's hearts transformed. As a result, one of our goals is for each student to recite the entire training course from memory. The "Review" section at the beginning of each study time helps learners to do just this. Please don't skip the review. In our experiences, even rice farmers educated to the third-grade level in Southeast Asia can repeat the entire content of *Making Radical Disciples* using the hand motions.

- *Build the Lesson:* When we train others, we "build" the lesson to aid in memory and confidence for the learners. For example, we ask the first question, read the scripture, give the answer, and show the hand motion. Then, we read the second question and follow the same process. Before we proceed to the third question, however, we review the question, answer, and hand motion for questions one and two. Then, we proceed to question three. We follow this same repetitive pattern throughout the lesson, "building up" the lesson with each new question. This helps learners to understand the whole lesson in context and remember it better.

- *Be an Example:* People do what they see modeled for them. Training is about living out the material ourselves and not merely teaching information to others. Fresh stories about how God is working in our own lives inspire those we train. Training is not a job; it is a lifestyle. Church-planting movements emerge in direct proportion to the number of believers in a people group who have adopted this attitude.

Simple Worship

Simple Worship is a critical component of Follow Jesus Training–one of the key skills for making disciples. Based on the Greatest Commandment, Simple Worship teaches people how to obey the command to love God with all their heart, all of their soul, all of their mind, and all of their strength.

We love God with all of our heart, so we worship Him. We love God with all of our soul, so we pray to Him. We love God with our whole mind, so we study the Bible. Finally, we love God with all our strength, so we practice what we have learned in order to share it with others.

God has blessed small groups all over Southeast Asia who have discovered they can have simple worship anywhere–homes, restaurants, at the park, in Sunday school, even at the Pagoda!

SCHEDULE

- A group of four will typically take about twenty minutes to complete a simple worship time.
- In a seminar setting, we have simple worship at the start of each day and after every lunch.
- The first time you do simple worship, model it for the group; take time to explain how to do each part.
- After you model how to do simple worship, ask each person in the training to choose a partner. Usually, learners choose a friend. When everyone has found their partner,

ask each pair to join with another pair–giving four people per group.

- Ask the groups to come up with their own "name", giving them a few minutes to do so; then go around the room and ask each group what their name is. Try to refer to the groups by this name throughout the rest of the training.

- In a weekly format, we like to teach people simple worship first. Each time we spend the entire time doing simple worship together. Then, we teach them the first two discipleship lessons the next two weeks. The following week, we share another simple worship practice session. In the same way, we rotate a simple worship training time and two *Making Radical Disciples* sessions, until we have completed the whole course. The group then moves to Track II - Simple Worship with Bible stories.

PROCESS

- Divide into groups of four.
- Each person takes a different part of simple worship.
- Each time you practice simple worship, learners rotate which part of simple worship they lead, so by the end of the training time they have done each part at least twice.

Worship

- One person leads the group in singing two choruses or hymns (depending upon your context).
- Instruments are not required.
- In the training session, ask learners to place their chairs as if they are sitting at a café table together.

- Every group will be singing different songs and that is good.
- Explain to the group that this is a time to worship God with all your heart as a group, not to see which group can sing the loudest.

Prayer

- *Another* person (different from the one who led worship) leads the group prayer time.
- The prayer leader asks each of the group members for a prayer request and writes it down.
- The prayer leader commits to pray for these items until the group meets again.
- After each person has shared their prayer request, the prayer leader prays for the group.

Study

- *Another* person in the group of four leads the group study time.
- The study leader tells a story from the Bible in his or her own words; we suggest stories from the Gospels, at least in the beginning.
- Depending on the group, you may ask study leaders to first read the Bible story and then tell it in their own words.
- After the study leader tells the Bible story, they ask their group three questions:

  1. What did this story teach us about God?
  2. What did this story teach us about people?
  3. What did I learn in this story that will help me follow Jesus?

- The group discusses each question together, until the study leader feels the discussion wane; then the leader moves to the next question.

Practice

- *Another* person in the group of four leads the group practice time.
- The practice leader helps the group review the lesson again and insures that everyone understands the lesson and can teach it to others.
- The practice leader tells the same Bible story that the study leader told.
- The practice leader asks the same questions that the study leader asked and the group discusses each question again.

Ending

- The simple worship group ends the time of worship by singing another worship song, or saying the Lord's Prayer together.

KEY PRINCIPLES TO REMEMBER

- Groups of four work best in simple worship. If you must make a group of five, only create one. Two groups of three people are better than one group of six.
- One of the keys to reproducibility in simple worship is each person taking a turn practicing one of the four parts: worship, prayer, study, or practice. Groups of four give support to people learning new skills and are not as threatening as a larger group.

- Encourage groups to worship in their heart language. If there are no singers in the group (which does happen), help the group by suggesting they read a Psalm aloud together.
- Make certain you allow enough time for the practice person to take the group through a practice session. The accountability in the practice time brings reproduction of simple worship groups. Without the practice section, the time turns into just another Bible study group. Is that what you really want?

Part 2

TRAINING

1

Welcome

Welcome opens the training sessions or seminar by introducing the trainers and learners. Trainers introduce learners to eight pictures of Jesus as the following: Soldier, Seeker, Shepherd, Sower, Son, Holy One, Servant, and Steward–with matching hand motions. Because people learn by listening, seeing, and doing, Follow Jesus Training incorporates each of these learning styles in every session.

The Bible says the Holy Spirit is our teacher; learners are encouraged to depend on the Spirit throughout the training. The session ends by opening a "tea shop" to provide a more relaxed atmosphere among trainers and learners, the kind of setting the disciples enjoyed with Jesus.

WORSHIP

- Ask someone to pray for God's presence and blessing.
- Sing two choruses or hymns together.

BEGINNING

Who are the Trainers?

Trainers and learners should be in a circle at the beginning of the opening session. If tables have been set up, have them removed beforehand.

- Trainers model how learners will introduce themselves.
- The Trainer and Apprentice introduce each other. They share the other person's name, information about their family, ethnic group (if appropriate), and a way that God has blessed them during the month.

Who are the Learners?

- Divide learners into pairs.
  Tell them, "You will now introduce each other in the same way that I and my apprentice just did."

- They should learn their partner's name, information about their family, ethnic group, and one way that God has blessed them the previous month. It may be helpful for them to write the information in their student notebook so they will not forget.
- After about five minutes, ask learner pairs to introduce themselves to at least five other partners in the same way that you introduced your partner to them.

Who is Jesus?

"We have introduced ourselves to you, and you have introduced yourselves to each other. Now, we would like to introduce you to Jesus. There are many pictures of Jesus in the Bible, but we are going to concentrate on the eight main ones."

EIGHT PICTURES OF JESUS IN THE BIBLE

- Draw a circle on the whiteboard and list the pictures of Christ. Have students repeat them in order several times–until they can say them from memory easily.

"Jesus is a Soldier, Seeker, Shepherd, Sower, Son, Holy One, Servant, and Steward."

🖐 Soldier
Raise sword.

🖐 Seeker
Look back and forth with hand above eyes.

🖐 Shepherd
Move arms towards your body as if you are gathering people.

🖐 Sower
Cast seeds with hands.

🖐 Son
Move hands towards mouth as if you are eating.

🖐 Holy One
Put hands in classic "praying hands" pose.

"Jesus is *the* Holy One; we are called to be Saints."

✋ Servant
   Wield a hammer.

✋ Steward
   Take money from shirt pocket or purse.

"A picture is worth a thousand words, and these Biblical pictures will give you deeper insight into walking 'with' Jesus. A picture gives us a clear vision and the ability to recognize when and how Jesus is working.

A father was reading the newspaper and his young son kept interrupting him, wanting to play. After several interruptions, the father made a puzzle out of one page of the newspaper by cutting it into pieces. He told his son to take the pieces, tape them together in the right order, and then he would play with him.

The father believed this would take his son a long time, giving the father ample time to read the rest of his newspaper. Instead, the son returned after 10 minutes with the 'puzzle' complete. When asked how he did it so quickly, the son replied, 'It was easy. There was a picture on the back, and when I put the picture together all of the letters on the other side came together, too.'

These eight pictures of Jesus will give you a clear vision as you walk with Jesus.

To follow someone means to copy the way that person does things. An apprentice copies his master to learn a trade.

Students become like their teachers. All of us copy someone. Whom we copy is who we become. In our training times, we will ask questions, look for the answer in the Bible, discover how Jesus walked, and practice following him."

What are the Three Ways We Learn Best?

"There are three ways that people learn. Everyone uses all three, but each of us tends to learn best one way. In this training, we will use all three ways people learn in each lesson, so each of you can master the material with your specific learning style.

Some people learn best by listening. For that reason, we will always read the scripture aloud and ask the questions aloud."

Listening
Cup your hand around your ear.

"Some people learn best by seeing. For that reason, we will use pictures and dramas to illustrate important truths."

Seeing
Point to your eyes.

"Some people learn best by doing. For that reason, we will have hands-on activities that will help you do what we are talking about and practice it."

Doing
Make a rolling motion with your hands.

46

"Listening, seeing, and doing are the three main teachers we have. The Bible also tells us that the Holy Spirit is the one who is our teacher. Throughout the seminar, I urge you to depend on the Holy Spirit to learn the lessons because he is the one who teaches best."

ENDING

The Tea Shop Is Open! ☙

"Which place do you enjoy more: a school classroom or a teashop (or coffee shop) with friends?

We learn many good things in the classroom, and we should respect our teachers. However, most of what we learn about our friends, family, and village is in the tea shop. This was true when Jesus walked on the earth, as well."

—Luke 7:31-35—Jesus went on to say: What are you people like? What kind of people are you? You are like children sitting in the market and shouting to each other, "We played the flute, but you would not dance! We sang a funeral song, but you would not cry!" John the Baptist did not go around eating and drinking, and you said, "John has a demon in him!" But because the Son of Man goes around eating and drinking, you say, "Jesus eats and drinks too much! He is even a friend of tax collectors and sinners." Yet Wisdom is shown to be right by what its followers do.(CEV)

"We are more relaxed in the tea shop. If Jesus walked on the earth again today, He would spend time in tea or coffee shops. He followed this pattern when He came the first time. For that reason, we are changing this room from a training center into a teashop."

- At this point, arrange for learners to be served tea, coffee, and some light refreshments.

The purpose of "The Tea Shop is Open!" is to create a training atmosphere that is relaxed and more informal. In other words, a group setting which is closer to the way that Jesus trained the disciples.

2

Multiply

Multiply introduces Jesus as a Steward: stewards want a good return on their time and treasure, and they desire to live with integrity. Learners gain a vision for fruitfulness by exploring 1) God's first command to mankind, 2) Jesus' last command to mankind, 3) the 222 Principle, and 4) the differences between the Sea of Galilee and Dead Sea.

The lesson ends with an active-learning skit that demonstrates the difference in "yield", or fruit, between training others and merely teaching them. Learners are challenged to train people how to worship, pray, study God's word, and minister to others. With this investment of time, treasure, and integrity, learners will be able to give Jesus an amazing gift when they see Him in Heaven.

WORSHIP

- Ask someone to pray for God's presence and blessing.
- Sing two choruses or hymns together.

PRAYER

- Arrange learners into pairs with someone they have not been a partner with before.
- Each learner shares with his or her partner the answer to the following question:

  How can I pray for you today?

- Partners pray together.

STUDY

Review

Each review session is the same. Ask learners to stand and recite previous lessons learned. Make sure they do the hand motions, too.

What Are Eight Pictures That Help Us Follow Jesus?
Soldier, Seeker, Shepherd, Sower, Son, Saint, Servant, Steward

Our Spiritual Life Is Like a Balloon

- Take a balloon, show it to the group, and explain,

  "Our spiritual life is like a balloon."

- As you blow up the balloon, explain that we receive blessings from God. Let air out of the balloon and say,

  "God gives to us, so we will give to others. We are blessed to be a blessing."

- Repeat this process several times demonstrating the "in and out" nature of spiritual life.

"Most of us, however, do not give what we receive, but we keep it for ourselves. Maybe we think that if we give it out, God will not refill us. Maybe we think it is too hard to give."

- Keep blowing up the balloon, but periodically let a small amount of air out because you "feel guilty." God has given so much to you, and you are not giving much to others. Finally, blow the balloon until it bursts.

"Our spiritual life is like this illustration. When someone teaches us a lesson, we should teach what we have learned to someone else. When we receive a blessing, we should bless others. When we do not do this, it causes big problems in our spiritual life! Not giving what we have received is the sure path to spiritual defeat."

What is Jesus Like?

—Matthew 6:20-21—But store up for yourselves treasures in heaven, where moth and rust do not destroy, and where thieves do not break in and steal. For where your treasure is, there your heart will be also.

"Jesus is a Steward. He talked about money, possessions, and our priorities more than any other topic. As a steward, Jesus has invested in us and is looking for a good return."

Steward
Pretend to take money from shirt pocket or purse.

51

What are Three Things a Steward Does?

—Matthew 25:14-28—For it is just like a man going on a journey. He called his own slaves and turned over his possessions to them. To one he gave five talents; to another, two; and to another, one—to each according to his own ability. Then he went on a journey. Immediately the man who had received five talents went, put them to work, and earned five more. In the same way, the man with two earned two more. But the man who had received one talent went off, dug a hole in the ground, and hid his master's money. After a long time the master of those slaves came and settled accounts with them. The man who had received five talents approached, presented five more talents, and said, "Master, you gave me five talents. Look, I've earned five more talents." His master said to him, "Well done, good and faithful slave! You were faithful over a few things; I will put you in charge of many things. Enter your master's joy!" Then the man with two talents also approached. He said, "Master, you gave me two talents. Look, I've earned two more talents." His master said to him, "Well done, good and faithful slave! You were faithful over a few things; I will put you in charge of many things. Enter your master's joy!" Then the man who had received one talent also approached and said, "Master, I know you. You're a difficult man, reaping where you haven't sown and gathering where you haven't scattered seed. So I was afraid and went off and hid your talent in the ground. Look, you have what is yours." But his master replied to him, "You evil, lazy slave! If you knew that I reap where I haven't sown and gather where I haven't scattered, then you should have deposited my money with the bankers. And when I returned I would have received my money back with interest. So take the talent from him and give it to the one who has 10 talents." (HCSB)

1. Stewards invest their treasure wisely.

   "Jesus tells a story of three servants put in charge of investing the master's money. Two of them invested the master's money wisely."

2. Stewards invest their time wisely.

   "Jesus wants us to put His Kingdom first on our agenda."

3. Stewards live with integrity.

   "As Jesus sees our integrity and honesty in little things, He will entrust us with more."

"Jesus is a steward, and He lives in us. When we follow Him, we will be stewards, too. We will invest our treasure and time wisely, and live with integrity."

What Was God's First Command to Man?

—*Genesis 1:28—God blessed them; and God said to them, "Be fruitful and multiply, and fill the earth, and subdue it; and rule over the fish of the sea and over the birds of the sky and over every living thing that moves on the earth." (NASB)*

"God told people to multiply and have physical children."

What Was Jesus' Last Command to Man?

—Mark 16:15—He said to them, "Go into all the world and preach the good news to all creation."

"Jesus told His disciples to multiply and have spiritual children."

How Can I Be Fruitful and Multiply?

—2 Timothy 2:2—The things which you have heard from me in the presence of many witnesses entrust these to faithful men who will be able to teach others also. (NASB)

"When we train others, as we have been trained, then God multiplies our lives. We call this the '222 Principle.' Jesus revealed Himself to Paul. Paul trained Timothy. Timothy trained faithful people who trained others as well. And all through history it has continued…until one day someone shared with you about Jesus!"

Sea of Galilee/Dead Sea ◌

- Draw the picture on the next page, step-by-step, as you teach each part of the illustration. The picture is the completed drawing.

  "There are the two seas located in the country of Israel. Do you know their names?"

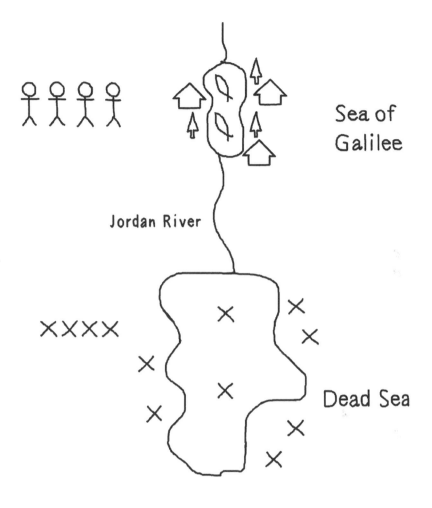

Sea of Galilee

Jordan River

Dead Sea

THE SEA OF GALILEE AND DEAD SEA

- Draw two circles, the smaller one on top. Connect them with a line. Draw a line upward from the top of the smaller circle. Label the two seas.

  "A river connects the Sea of Galilee and the Dead Sea. Do you know its name?"

THE JORDAN RIVER

- Label the river.

"The Sea of Galilee and the Dead Sea are very different. The Sea of Galilee has many fish."

- Draw fish in the Sea of Galilee.

"The Dead Sea has no fish."

- Draw Xs in the Dead Sea.

"The Sea of Galilee has many trees growing near it."

- Draw trees around the Sea of Galilee.

"The Dead Sea has no trees nearby."

- Draw Xs around the Dead Sea.

"The Sea of Galilee has many villages."

- Draw houses around the Sea of Galilee.

"The Dead Sea has no villages."

- Draw Xs around the Dead Sea.

"Four famous people lived by the Sea of Galilee. Do you know their names?"

PETER, ANDREW, JAMES, JOHN

- Draw four stick figures beside the Sea of Galilee.

"No famous people lived by the Dead Sea."

- Draw four Xs beside the Dead Sea.

"Why do you think the Dead Sea is 'dead' and the Sea of Galilee is 'living'?

Because the sea of Galilee has water coming in and out, whereas the dead sea only has water flowing in.

This is a picture of our spiritual life. When we receive a blessing, we should give a blessing. When we receive teaching, we should teach others. Then, we are like the Sea of Galilee. If we keep it to ourselves, we are like the Dead Sea.

Which sea is it *easier* to be like—the Dead Sea or Sea of Galilee? Most people are like the Dead Sea because they would rather receive than give. However, those who follow Jesus are like the Sea of Galilee. Jesus gave others what He had received from His Father. When we train others to train others, we are following Jesus' example.

Which sea do you want to be like? I want to be like the Sea of Galilee."

Memory Verse

–John 15:8–This is to my Father's glory, that you bear much fruit, showing yourselves to be my disciples.

- Everyone stands and says the memory verse ten times together. The first six times, learners use their Bible or student notes. The last four times, they say the verse from memory. Learners should say the verse reference before each time they quote the verse, and sit down when finished.
- Following this routine will help the trainers know what team has finished the lesson in the "Practice" section.

PRACTICE

- Ask learners to sit facing their prayer partner for this session. Partners take turns teaching each other the lesson.

"The *youngest* person in the pair will be the leader."

- This simply means that they will train first.
- Follow the *Training Trainers Process* on page 9.
- Emphasize that you want them to teach everything in the "Study" section exactly the way you did.

"Ask the questions, read the scriptures together, and answer the questions the same way that I did with you.

Draw the Sea of Galilee/Dead Sea illustration and quote the memory verse the same way that I did with you.

Each of you should use a clean sheet of paper every time you draw the Sea of Galilee/Dead Sea illustration."

- After teaching each other the lesson, ask learners to think of someone they will share this lesson with after the training. Have them write the person's name at the top of the first page of the lesson.

ENDING

"A Gift for Jesus" Skit ✺

- Ask someone to volunteer to help with a skit.
- If you have a small group, draw stick figures on the whiteboard instead of performing the skit. Station the volunteer on one side of the room and yourself on the other side.
- Explain that you want everyone to imagine that both you and the volunteer have the same spiritual maturity.
- Both you and the volunteer:

✋ Praise
Raise hands in worship to God.

✋ Pray
Put hands in classic prayer pose.

✋ Study the Bible
Put palms upward as if you are reading a book.

✋ Tell others about Jesus
Put hand out as if you are spreading seeds.

- Emphasize that you are the same spiritually, except for one difference.
- Explain that the only difference between you and the volunteer is that he or she trains the people he wins to Christ to train others. You only teach the people you lead to Christ. You do not train them to train others.

"Now, I want to show you the difference that training makes."

- Explain that each year both you and the volunteer reach one person for Christ.
- Both you and the volunteer go into the audience, get one person, bring them back to your station, and have them stand with you.

"You can see after one year, there is no difference. I have one person here, and he has one person over there."

- However, only the volunteer trains the person he leads to Christ. Perform the same hand motions; this time, both of them practice the hand motions together. You perform the hand motions by yourself.

"Let's see what happens in year two. Both he and I win someone to Christ. The only difference is that he trains his people to do the same. So this year, I will get my one person, but both of them in the other group will get a person."

- Both you and the volunteer go into the audience to choose your next disciples. Then, the trainer's disciple also gets a disciple.

"You can see after two years that there is still little difference: I have two people, he has three."

- Again, the volunteer and the three people with him/her practice the hand motions, but you are the only one in your group who does the hand motions.
- Repeat this process for several "years" until all of the people in the training have been chosen. Each time you do the actions alone and tell your converts they should praise, pray, study God's word, and share the good news.
- At some point, you will no longer have enough people. In that case, tell people that if they cannot get another disciple, raise two hands to show that they are two people now.
- By year five, learners will be impressed with the number of people trained by the volunteer compared to the number taught by you. Emphasize repeatedly that you really love your disciples and want them to be strong, so you teach them many things, but you never train them to train others.

"When you get to Heaven, what kind of present do you want to give Jesus for dying on the cross for you?–Just a handful of people like I have, or a great number of disciples like him(or her)?"

- Point to the volunteer on the other side of the room.

"God has commanded us to be fruitful and multiply. I want to be like Jesus, training others who train others. I want to give Jesus a big present of many people whom I have trained and then who have trained others. I want to be a steward of my treasure and time, and I want to live with integrity."

- Ask your group to join with the other group and train each other so everyone can be a winner.
- Ask the volunteer from the skit "A Gift for Jesus" to close the session in prayer.

3

Love

Love introduces Jesus as a Shepherd: shepherds lead, protect, and feed their sheep. We "feed" people when we teach them from God's Word, but what should be the first thing we teach people about God? Learners explore the most important commandment, identify who the source of love is, and discover how to worship based on the most important commandment.

Learners practice leading a simple disciple group with four key elements: worship (loving God with the whole heart), prayer (loving God with all the soul), Bible study (loving God with the all the mind), and practicing a skill (so we can love God with all our strength). A final skit, "Sheep and Tigers," demonstrates the need for many disciple groups among believers.

WORSHIP

- Ask someone to pray for God's presence and blessing.
- Sing two choruses or hymns together.

PRAYER

- Arrange learners into pairs with someone they have not been a partner with before.
- Each learner shares with their partner the answer to the following questions:

  1. How can we pray for lost people you know to be saved?
  2. How can we pray for the group you are training?

- If a partner has not started training anyone, pray for potential people in their sphere of influence who they can begin to train.
- Partners pray together.

STUDY

Review

Each review session is the same. Ask learners to stand and recite previous lessons learned. Make sure they do the hand motions, too.

What Are Eight Pictures That Help Us Follow Jesus?
Soldier, Seeker, Shepherd, Sower, Son, Saint, Servant, Steward

Multiply
What are three things a steward does?
What was God's first command to man?
What was Jesus' last command to man?
How can I be fruitful and multiply?
What are the names of the two seas located in Israel?
Why are they so different?
Which one do you want to be like?

64

What is Jesus Like?

—Mark 6:34—When Jesus went ashore, He saw a large crowd, and He felt compassion for them because they were like sheep without a shepherd; and He began to teach them many things. (NASB)

"Jesus is the good Shepherd. He loved the great multitude, saw their problems, and began to teach them the ways of God. He lives in us and does the same through our lives."

 Shepherd
Move hands towards your body as if you are gathering people.

What are Three Things a Shepherd Does?

—Psalm 23:1-6—The LORD is my shepherd, I shall not want. He makes me lie down in green pastures; He leads me beside quiet waters. He restores my soul; He guides me in the paths of righteousness For His name's sake. Even though I walkthrough the valley of the shadow of death, I fear no evil, for You are with me; Your rod and Your staff, they comfort me. You prepare a table before me in the presence of my enemies; You have anointed my head with oil; my cup overflows. Surely goodness and loving-kindness will follow me all the days of my life, and I will dwell in the house of the LORD forever. (NASB)

1. Shepherds lead their sheep on the right path.
2. Shepherds protect their sheep.
3. Shepherds feed their sheep.

"Jesus is a shepherd, and as we follow Him, we will be shepherds, too. We will lead people to Jesus, protect people from evil, and feed them from God's Word."

What is the Most Important Command to Teach Others?

—Mark 12:28-31—One of the teachers of the law came and heard them debating. Noticing that Jesus had given them a good answer, he asked him, "Of all the commandments, which is the most important?" "The most important one," answered Jesus, "is this: 'Hear, O Israel, the Lord our God, the Lord is one. Love the Lord your God with all your heart and with all your soul and with all your mind and with all your strength.' The second is this: 'Love your neighbor as yourself.' There is no commandment greater than these."

LOVE GOD

Put hands upwards towards God.

LOVE PEOPLE

Put hands outwards towards others.

Where Does Love Come From?

—I John 4:7, 8—Dear friends, let us love one another, because love is from God, and everyone who loves has been born of God and knows God. The one who does not love does not know God, because God is love. (HCSB)

LOVE COMES FROM GOD

"Therefore…we receive love from God, and we give love back to him."

✋ Put hands upwards as if you are receiving loveand then give the love back to God.

"We receive love from God, and we give it to other people."

✋ Put hands upwards as if you are receiving love, then spread hands out as if you are giving it to others.

What is Simple Worship?

✋ Praise

Lift hands in praise to God.

✋ Prayer

Put hands in classic "praying hands" pose.

✋ Study

Put hands palms upward as if you are reading a book.

✋ Practice

Move hand back and forth as if you are casting seeds.

Why Do We Have Simple Worship?

—Mark 12:30–Love the Lord your God with all your heart, and with all your soul, and with all your mind, and with all your strength.

We…	So We…	Hand motions
Love God with all our Heart	Praise	Put hand over heart and then raise hands up in praise to God.
Love God with all our Soul	Pray	Clutch hands to sides and then put hands in classic prayer pose.
Love God with all our Mind	Study	Put hand on the right side of the head as if thinking, and then put palms upward as if you are reading a book.
Love God with all our Strength	Share What We Have Learned	Put arms up and flex muscles, then put hand out spreading seeds.

- Review the Simple Worship outline with learners. Each part of Simple Worship trains us to obey the most important commandment of Jesus, found in Mark 12:30.
- This lesson explains the purpose of Simple Worship. Practice the hand motions with learners several times.

"We love God with all of our heart, so we worship; we love God with all of our soul, so we pray; we love God with all of our mind, so we study; we love God with all of our strength, so we practice."

How Many People Does It Take to Have Simple Worship?

—Matthew 18:20—For where two or three come together in my name, there am I with them.

"Jesus promised that where two or three believers are together, He is there with them."

Memory Verse

—John 13:34, 35—So now I am giving you a new commandment: Love each other. Just as I have loved you, you should love each other. Your love for one another will prove to the world that you are my disciples. (NLT)

- Everyone stands and says the memory verse ten times together. The first six times, learners use their Bible or student notes. The last four times, they say the verse from memory. Learners should say the reference of the verse each time before they quote the verse and sit down when finished.

- This will help the trainers know who has finished the lesson in the "Practice" section.

PRACTICE

- Ask learners to sit facing their prayer partner for this session. Partners take turns teaching each other the lesson.

"The *older person* in the pair will be the leader."

- Follow the *Training Trainers Process* on page 9.
- Emphasize how you want them to teach everything in the "Study" section exactly the way you did.

"Ask the questions, read the scriptures together, and answer the questions the same way that I did with you."

- After the learners have practiced training each other the lesson, ask learners to think about someone that they will share this lesson with outside the training.

"Take a few moments to think about someone you can teach this lesson to outside of this training. Write that person's name at the top of the first page of this lesson."

ENDING

Simple Worship

- Divide learners into groups of four. Give each group of four, one minute to come up with a name for their group.

- Go around the room and ask groups to tell the name they have chosen.
- Review the steps in Simple Worship with the learners, telling them they are going to practice Simple Worship together.
- Each person in the Simple Worship group should lead a different part in the worship time. For example, one person leads the worship time, another the prayer time, another the Bible story time, and another the Practice time.
- Tell the groups to lead the worship time softly as there will be other groups nearby. Remind learners not to "preach" but "tell" the Bible story. Ask the "Bible story person" to tell their group a story about God's love. Suggest the story of the prodigal son, if learners cannot decide which Bible story to share.
- The "Practice" person asks the three study questions.

1. What does this story tell us about God?
2. What does this story tell us about people?
3. How will this story help me follow Jesus?

Why is it Important for You to Start a Disciple Group?

SHEEP AND TIGERS ☙

- Explain that the room is a sheep farm. Ask one volunteer to be a guard (shepherd) for the sheep. Ask three volunteers to be tigers. Everyone else is a sheep.

"The goal of the game is for the tigers to hurt as many sheep as they can. If the guard touches a tiger, then the tiger must crouch down and is 'dead.' If a tiger touches a sheep, then the sheep must crouch down and be 'hurt.' The guard can be hurt if two tigers touch him/her at the same time. Once any participant is 'hurt' or 'dead,' you are out of play until the game is over."

- Ask the group to remove books, pencils, and other potentially dangerous items from the floor before they begin.

"Some of you may scream during the game and that is O.K."

- Count to three and say "Go!" Let the game continue until all the tigers are dead or all the sheep are hurt. Most, if not all of the sheep will be hurt. The guard may be hurt as well.
- Tell the group that you are going to play the game again. This time; however, choose five additional guards and keep the same three tigers as before. Everyone else is a sheep. Encourage sheep to huddle close to a guard in small groups for protection. Count to three and say "Go!"
- Let the game continue until all the tigers are dead or all the sheep are hurt. All of the tigers should die rather quickly. A few sheep may be hurt.

"This is a picture of why we need many new groups and churches. The first game is like one pastor who tries to protect his whole church and wants it to grow bigger and bigger. It is easy for Satan to come and hurt many of the members. In the second game, several spiritual leaders were able to protect their small groups. Because of this, Satan and his demons (the tigers) were not able to hurt the sheep as easily."

"Jesus is the Good Shepherd. He gave His life for the sheep. We, as shepherds in spirit, should be willing to give our 'lives'—our time, our prayer, our focus—to those who are our sheep, those who are looking to us to learn about Jesus. We can only be there for so many people at one time, right? Only Jesus is omnipresent. This is another reason that we should teach others to teach others, so that there are more to bear one another's burdens and so fulfill the law of Christ."

4

Pray

Pray introduces learners to Jesus as the Holy One. He lived a holy life and died for us on the cross. God commands us to be saints as we follow Jesus. A Saint worships God, lives a holy life, and prays for others. Following Jesus' example in prayer, we praise God, repent of our sins, ask God for the things we need, and yield to what He asks us to do.

God answers our prayers in one of four ways: no (if we ask with wrong motives), slow (if the timing is not right), grow (if we need to develop more maturity before He gives the answer), or go (when we pray according to His Word and will). Learners memorize God's phone number, 3-3-3, based on Jeremiah 33:3 and are encouraged to "call" God every day.

WORSHIP

- Ask someone to pray for God's presence and blessing.
- Sing two choruses or hymns together.

PRAYER

- Arrange learners into pairs with someone they have not been a partner with before.
- Each learner shares with their partner the answer to the following questions:

  1. How can we pray for lost people you know to be saved?
  2. How can we pray for the group you are training?

- If a partner has not started training anyone, pray for potential people in their sphere of influence they can begin to train.
- Partners pray together.

STUDY

Telephone Game ∞

"Have you ever played the telephone game?"

- Explain that you will tell the person beside you a few words, and then they will tell the next person. Each person whispers to their neighbor what they have heard until it goes around the circle.
- The last person will repeat the phrase they heard. You will say the phrase you said at first, and everyone can compare how similar the phrases are. Choose a phrase that is a little silly and has several parts to it. Play the game twice.

"We often hear many things about God, but we do not always talk to Him directly. In our game, if you had asked me what I had said, it would not have been difficult to understand. When you heard the phrase after it had gone through several people, though, it was easy to make mistakes. Prayer is very important in our spiritual life because it is talking *directly* to God."

Review

Each review session is the same. Ask learners to stand and recite previous lessons learned. Make sure they do the hand motions, too.

What Are Eight Pictures That Help Us Follow Jesus?
Soldier, Seeker, Shepherd, Sower, Son, Saint, Servant, Steward

Multiply
What are three things a steward does?
What was God's first command to man?
What was Jesus' last command to man?
How can I be fruitful and multiply?
What are the two seas located in Israel?
Why are they so different?
Which one do you want to be like?

Love
What are three things a shepherd does?
What is the most important command to teach others?
Where does love come from?
What is simple worship?
Why do we have simple worship?
How many people does it take to have simple worship?

What is Jesus Like?

—Luke 4:33-35—In the synagogue there was a man possessed by a demon, an evil spirit. He cried out at the top of his voice, "Ha! What do you want with us, Jesus of Nazareth? Have you come to destroy us? I know who you are—the Holy One of God!" "Be quiet!" Jesus said sternly. "Come out of him!" Then the demon threw the man down before them all and came out without injuring him.

"Jesus is the Holy One of God. He is the one we worship. He also intercedes for us before the throne of God. As Jesus' followers, we worship Him. He calls us to intercede on behalf of others and live a holy life connected to Him. Jesus is the Holy One. We are called to be saints."

Saint
Put hands in classic "praying hands" pose

What are Three Things a Saint Does?

—Matthew 21:12-16—Jesus entered the temple area and drove out all who were buying and selling there. He overturned the tables of the money changers and the benches of those selling doves. "It is written," he said to them, "'My house will be called a house of prayer,' but you are making it a 'den of robbers.'" The blind and the lame came to him at the temple, and he healed them. But when the chief priests and the teachers of the law saw the wonderful things he did and the children shouting in the temple area, "Hosanna to the Son of David," they were indignant. "Do you hear what these children are saying?" they asked him. "Yes," replied Jesus, "have you never read, 'From the lips of children and infants you have ordained praise'?"

1. Saints worship God.

   "We are to praise God as the children did in the temple."

2. Saints live a holy life.

   "Jesus did not allow his father's house to be polluted by greed."

3. Saints pray for others.

   "Jesus said God's house is a house of prayer."

"Jesus is the Holy One and lives in us. As we follow Him, we will grow in holiness as His saints. We will worship, live a holy life, and pray for others just like Jesus did."

How Should We Pray?

—Luke 10:21—At that very time He rejoiced greatly in the Holy Spirit, and said, "I praise You, O Father, Lord of heaven and earth, that You have hidden these things from the wise and intelligent and have revealed them to infants. Yes, Father, for this way was well pleasing in Your sight." (NASB)

PRAISE

"Jesus came to God in prayer, rejoicing and giving thanks for what God was doing in the world."

Praise
Hands raised in worship.

—Luke 18:13, 14—The tax collector stood off at a distance and did not think he was good enough even to look up toward heaven. He was so sorry for what he had done that he pounded his chest and prayed, "God, have pity on me! I am such a sinner." Then Jesus said, "When the two men went home, it was the tax collector and not the Pharisee who was pleasing to God. If you put yourself above others, you will be put down. But if you humble yourself, you will be honored." (CEV)

REPENT

"In this story, Jesus contrasts two men who were praying. When the Pharisee prayed, he was proud and considered himself above 'sinners'. When the tax collector prayed, he humbled himself before God and confessed his sinful condition. Jesus said the tax collector was the one who pleased God in prayer.

Repentance means admitting our sin and turning away from doing it again. Those who repent are forgiven and please God."

Repent
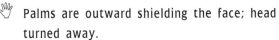 Palms are outward shielding the face; head turned away.

—Luke 11:9—So I say to you, keep asking, and it will be given to you. Keep searching, and you will find. Keep knocking, and the door will be opened to you. (HCSB)

ASK

"After having entered God's presence with praise and repenting of our sins, we are ready to ask God for the things we need. Many people start their prayers by asking, but this is rude."

Ask
 Hands cupped to receive.

—*Luke 22:42–Father, if You are willing, take this cup away from Me—nevertheless, not My will, but Yours, be done. (HCSB)*

YIELD

"Jesus agonized in the Garden of Gethsemane about going to the cross. Yet, he said, 'Nevertheless, not my will, but yours be done.' After asking God for the things we need, we listen to him and yield to the things he asks from us."

Yield - God asks us
 Hands folded in prayer and placed high on the forehead to symbolize respect.

Praying Together

• Lead the group in a time of prayer using the four parts of prayer, one section at a time.

- Everyone in the group prays aloud during the 'Praise' and 'Ask' sections. Pray silently during the 'Repent' and 'Yield' sections.

  "You will know when the time is up for that section when I say, 'And all God's people said...Amen.'"

- Encourage learners to use the hand motions as they pray to help them remember which part of prayer they are practicing.

How Will God Answer Us?

> *—Matthew 20:20-22—Then the mother of James and John, the sons of Zebedee, came to Jesus with her sons. She knelt respectfully to ask a favor. "What is your request?" he asked. She replied, "In your Kingdom, please let my two sons sit in places of honor next to you, one on your right and the other on your left." But Jesus answered by saying to them, "You don't know what you are asking! Are you able to drink from the bitter cup of suffering I am about to drink?" "Oh yes," they replied, "we are able!" (NLT)*

NO

"The mother of James and John asked Jesus to give her sons the most privileged positions in Jesus' kingdom. Pride and power motivated her. Jesus told her that he would not grant her request because only the Father had that authority. God says 'no' when we ask with the wrong motives."

No - We have the wrong motives.
  Shake head signaling "no."

—John 11:11-15—After he had said this, he went on to tell them, "Our friend Lazarus has fallen asleep; but I am going there to wake him up." His disciples replied, "Lord, if he sleeps, he will get better." Jesus had been speaking of his death, but his disciples thought he meant natural sleep. So then he told them plainly, "Lazarus is dead, and for your sake I am glad I was not there, so that you may believe. But let us go to him."

SLOW

"Jesus knew that Lazarus was sick, and he could have arrived much earlier and healed him. However, Jesus waited until Lazarus was dead because he wanted to do a greater work—a resurrection. Jesus knew that it would strengthen their faith and bring greater glory to God if Lazarus rose again. Sometimes we must wait because the time is not right."

> Slow - We need to wait on God's timing and
> not our own.
>  Hands push down like slowing a car.

—Luke 9:51-56—As the time drew near for him to ascend to heaven, Jesus resolutely set out for Jerusalem. He sent messengers ahead to a Samaritan village to prepare for his arrival. But the people of the village did not want Jesus to stay there. When James and John saw this, they said to Jesus, "Lord, should we call down fire from heaven to burn them up?" But Jesus turned and rebuked them. So they went on to another village. (NLT)

GROW

"When the Samaritan village did not welcome Jesus, James and John wanted Him to destroy the entire village with fire. The disciples did not understand Jesus' mission: He came to save people, not to harm them. The disciples had some growing up to do! In a similar way, when we ask God for things that we do not really need, or would get us in trouble, or do not line up with God's mission for our lives, He does not give them. He says we need to grow."

Grow - God wants us to grow in an area first.
 Hands outline a plant growing up.

—John 15:7—But if you remain in me, and my words remain in you, you may ask for anything you want, and it will be granted! (NLT)

GO

"When we follow Jesus and live by His words, we can ask God for the things we need and be confident He will give them. God says, "Yes! Go! You can have it!""

Go - We have prayed according to His will and He says "yes."
 Head nodding, signaling "yes" and hands moving forward signaling, "go".

Pray

Memory Verse

> *–Luke 11:9–So I say to you, keep asking, and it will be given to you. Keep searching, and you will find. Keep knocking, and the door will be opened to you. (HCSB)*

- Everyone stands and says the memory verse ten times together. The first six times, learners use their Bible or student notes. The last four times, they say the verse from memory. Learners should say the verse's reference before they quote the verse each time and sit down when finished.
- This will help the trainers know who has finished the lesson in the "Practice" section.

PRACTICE

- Ask learners to sit facing their prayer partner for this session. Partners take turns teaching each other the lesson.

"The shorter person in the pair will be the leader."

- Follow the *Training Trainers Process* on page 9.
- Emphasize that you want them to teach everything in the "Study" section exactly the way you did.

"Ask the questions, read the scriptures together, and answer the questions the same way that I did with you."

- After the learners have practiced training each other the lesson, ask learners to think about someone that they will share this lesson with outside the training.

"Take a few moments to think about someone you can teach this lesson to outside of this training. Write that person's name at the top of the first page of this lesson."

ENDING

God's Phone Number ✿

"Do you know God's phone number? It is 3-3-3."

—Jeremiah 33:3—Call to Me and I will answer you, and I will tell you great and mighty things, which you do not know. (NASB)

"Make sure you call Him every day. He is waiting to hear from you and loves to talk to His children!"

Two Hands, Ten Fingers ✿

* Hold up two hands.

  "There are two kinds of people for whom we should pray every day: believers and unbelievers.

  We pray for believers that they will follow Jesus and train others to do the same. We pray for unbelievers that they will receive Christ."

* Encourage learners to choose five people to count on their right hand who are not believers yet. Spend time praying for them to become followers of Jesus.
* On the left hand, learners should include believers they know whom they can train to follow Jesus. Spend time praying for these believers to follow Jesus with all of their heart.

5

Obey

Obey introduces learners to Jesus as a Servant: servants help people; they have a humble heart, and they obey their master. In the same way Jesus served and followed His Father, we now serve and follow Jesus. As the one with all authority, He has given us four commands to obey: go, make disciples, baptize, and teach them to obey all He has commanded. Jesus also promised that He would always be with us. When Jesus gives a command, we should obey it all of the time, immediately, and from a heart of love.

Storms in life come to everyone, but the wise man builds his life obeying Jesus' commands; the foolish man does not. Finally, learners begin an Acts 29 Map, a picture of their harvest field, which they will present at the end of the Discipleship Seminar.

WORSHIP

- Ask someone to pray for God's presence and blessing.
- Sing two choruses or hymns together.

PRAYER

- Arrange learners into pairs with someone they have not been a partner with before.
- Each learner shares with their partner the answer to the following questions:

  1. How can we pray for lost people you know to be saved?
  2. How can we pray for the group you are training?

- If a partner has not started training anyone, pray for potential people in their sphere of influence they can begin to train.
- Partners pray together.

STUDY

Do The Funky Chicken! ☙

"I am going to do something today I hope you never forget. Stand in a circle and look at me. I want you to imitate everything I do."

- The first time, demonstrate simple hand motions that everyone can copy. Examples include yawning, patting your cheek, rubbing your elbow, etc. Do them slowly and simply enough that everyone can easily do them.

"Was it easy to follow me? Why or why not?

It was easy to copy me because I did everything simply. Now, I want you to copy me again. Remember, do everything exactly the way I do it."

- The second time, demonstrate motions which are a combination of the Funky Chicken dance, John Travolta doing disco, and the fox trot. Make up your own crazy, complicated dance that no one can copy. Some will try to imitate you, but most will just laugh and say it is impossible.

"Was it easy to follow me that time? Why or why not?

We are teaching you lessons that are easy to reproduce. When we teach lessons this way, you can train others who will train others. When a lesson is too complicated, people cannot share it with others. When you study the way Jesus taught, you find that He shared simple lessons people could remember and tell others. We want to follow Jesus' method when we train others."

Review

Each review session is the same. Ask learners to stand and recite previous lessons learned. Make sure they do the hand motions, too.

What Are Eight Pictures That Help Us Follow Jesus?
Soldier, Seeker, Shepherd, Sower, Son, Saint, Servant, Steward

Multiply
What are three things a steward does?
What was God's first command to man?
What was Jesus' last command to man?
How can I be fruitful and multiply?
What are the two seas located in Israel?
Why are they so different?
Which one do you want to be like?

Love

> *What are three things a shepherd does?*
> *What is the most important command to teach others?*
> *Where does love come from?*
> *What is simple worship?*
> *Why do we have simple worship?*
> *How many people does it take to have simple worship?*

Pray

> *What are three things a saint does?*
> *How should we pray?*
> *How will God answer us?*
> *What is God's phone number?*

What is Jesus Like?

> *—Mark 10:45—For even the Son of Man came not to be served, but to serve others, and to give his life as a ransom for many. (NLT)*

"Jesus is a Servant. The passion of Jesus was to serve His Father by giving His life for mankind."

> **Servant**
> Pretend to hammer.

What are Three Things a Servant Does?

> *—Philippians 2:5-8—Your attitude should be the same as that of Christ Jesus: Who, being in very nature God, did not consider equality with God something to be grasped, but made himself nothing, taking the very nature of a*

servant, being made in human likeness. And being found
in appearance as a man, he humbled himself and became
obedient to death—even death on a cross!

1. Servants help others.

    "Jesus died on the cross to help us come back to
    the family of God."

2. Servants have a humble heart.
3. Servants obey their master.

    "Jesus obeyed the Father. We must obey our master."

"Jesus helped us by dying on the cross for our sins. He
humbled Himself and always sought to obey His Father.
Jesus is a servant and lives in us. As we follow Him, we will
be servants, too. We will help others, have a humble heart,
and obey our master—Jesus."

Who Has The Highest Authority in the World?

—Matthew 28:18—Then Jesus came to them and said, "All
authority in heaven and on earth has been given to me."

"Jesus is the highest authority in Heaven and on earth.
He has more authority than our parents, teachers, and
government officials. In fact, He has more authority and
power than everyone on the earth put together does.
Because He has the highest authority, when He gives us a
command, we should obey Him before anyone else."

What Are Four Commands Jesus Has Given Every Believer?

—Matthew 28:19-20a—Therefore go and make disciples of all nations, baptizing them in the name of the Father and of the Son and of the Holy Spirit, and teaching them to obey everything I have commanded you.

GO

🖐 Move fingers forward "walking."

MAKE DISCIPLES

🖐 Use all four hand motions from Simple Worship: praise, pray, study, practice.

BAPTIZE THEM

🖐 Put your hand on your other elbow; move the elbow up and down as if someone is being baptized.

TEACH THEM TO OBEY HIS COMMANDS

🖐 Put hands together as if you are reading a book, and then move the "book" back and forth from left to right as if you are teaching people.

How Should We Obey Jesus?

"I want to share three stories with you that illustrate the kind of obedience God desires from us. Please listen closely so you can repeat them when you teach the lesson to your partner in a few minutes."

ALL THE TIME

"A son told his dad he would obey him every month of the year except for one. During that month, he would do whatever he liked (drink alcohol, stop going to school, etc.). What do you think the dad said?

The same boy told his dad, 'I will obey you every week of the year, but for one week I will do whatever I wish.' (Do drugs, run away from home, etc.) What do you think the dad said?

Then, the boy said, 'I will obey you every day of the year, except one. On that one day I will do whatever I want.' (Get married; murder someone, etc.) What do you think the dad said?

We expect our children to obey all of the time. In the same way, when Jesus gives us a command, He expects us to obey Him all of the time."

All of the time
Move right hand from your left side to right side.

IMMEDIATELY

"There was a girl who loved her mother very much. Her mother became very sick and was about to die. The mother asked her daughter, 'Please, get me a drink of water.' The daughter said, 'Yes, I will… (short pause) next week.' What do you think the mother said?

We expect our children to obey immediately, not at their convenience. In the same way, when Jesus gives us a command, He expects us to obey Him immediately, not sometime in the future."

Immediately
Move hands top to bottom in a slicing motion.

FROM A HEART OF LOVE

"There was a young man who wanted to get married. I told him I would make a robot that obeyed his every command. When he came home from work, the robot would say, 'I love you so much; you are such a hard worker.' If he asked his robot wife to do anything, she would always say, 'Yes, honey. You are the greatest man in the world.' What do you think my friend thought about this kind of wife? (Imitate a robot when you say what the robot would say.)

We want love to come from a true heart, not from a programmed robot. We want true love. In the same way, God wants us to obey from a heart of love."

From a heart of love
Cross hands over the chest and then raise hands in praise to God.

- Review the three hand motions several times:

"Jesus wants us to obey Him: all the time, immediately, from a heart of love.

Jesus has given every believer four commands. How should we obey?"

HE COMMANDED US TO GO.

👋 Move fingers forward "walking."

HOW SHOULD WE OBEY?

"All the time, immediately, from a heart of love."

HE COMMANDED US TO MAKE DISCIPLES.

👋 Use all four hand motions from Simple Worship: praise, pray, study, practice.

HOW SHOULD WE OBEY?

"All the time, immediately, from a heart of love."

HE COMMANDED US TO BAPTIZE THEM

👋 Put your hand on your other elbow; move the elbow up and down as if someone is being baptized.

HOW SHOULD WE OBEY?

"All the time, immediately, from a heart of love."

HE COMMANDED US TO TEACH THEM TO OBEY
HIS COMMANDS.

🖐 Put hands together as if you are reading a book,
and then move the "book" back and forth in a
semi-circle as if you are teaching people.

HOW SHOULD WE OBEY?

"All the time, immediately, from a heart of love."

What Did Jesus Promise Every Believer?

*—Matthew 28:20b—And surely I am with you always, to
the very end of the age.*

"Jesus is always with us. He is with us here, now."

Memory Verse

*—John 15:10—When you obey my commandments, you
remain in my love, just as I obey my Father's commandments
and remain in his love.(NLT)*

- Everyone stands and says the memory verse ten times
  together. The first six times, learners use their Bible or
  student notes. The last four times, they say the verse from
  memory. Learners should say the reference before each
  time they quote the verse and sit down when finished.
- This will help the trainers know who has finished the
  lesson in the "Practice" section.

PRACTICE

- Ask learners to sit facing their prayer partner for this session. Partners take turns teaching each other the lesson.

"The *tallest person* in the pair will be the leader."

- Follow the *Training Trainers Process* on page 9.
- Emphasize that you want them to teach everything in the "Study" section exactly the way you did.

"Ask the questions, read the Scriptures together, and answer the questions the same way that I did with you."

- After the learners have practiced training each other the lesson, ask learners to think about someone that they will share this lesson with outside the training.
"Take a few moments to think about someone you can teach this lesson to outside of this training. Write that person's name at the top of the first page of this lesson."

ENDING

Building On the True Foundation ❧

- Ask for three volunteers for the next skit: two to perform the skit and one to be the narrator. Place the two volunteers in front of you and the narrator off to the side. The two volunteers performing the skit should be men.
- Ask the narrator to read Matthew 7:24, 25

"The wise man built his house on the rock."

—Mathew 7:24, 25—Anyone who hears and obeys these teachings of mine is like a wise person who built a house on solid rock. Rain poured down, rivers flooded, and winds beat against that house. But it did not fall, because it was built on solid rock. (CEV)

- After the narrator reads the passage, explain what happened to the wise man, making a sound like wind while pouring water on the head of the first volunteer.
- Hide the water bottle nearby before the skit.
- Ask the narrator to read Matthew 7:26, 27

"The foolish man built his house on the sand."

—Matthew 7:26, 27—Anyone who hears my teachings and doesn't obey them is like a foolish person who built a house on sand. The rain poured down, the rivers flooded, and the winds blew and beat against that house. Finally, it fell with a crash. (CEV)

- After the narration, explain what happened to the foolish man, making a sound like wind while pouring water on the head of the second volunteer. He should fall down at the end of the skit as you say, "And great was the fall of that house."

"When we obey Jesus' commands, we are like the wise man. When we do not, we are like the foolish man. We want to make sure that the people we are training, base their lives on obeying Jesus commands. His word is a solid foundation in the difficulties of life."

Acts 29 Map - Part 1 ∝

- After the "true foundation" skit, give each learner a piece of poster paper, pens, pencils, color pencils, crayons, markers, etc.

- Explain that everyone is going to make a map of the place where God has called him or her to go. There will be several times during the training that they can work on their map. They can work on them during the evenings as well. This map represents their obedience to Jesus' command to go.
- Ask learners to draw a map of the place God has called them to go. Their map should include roads, rivers, mountains, landmarks, etc.

Possible Map Symbols

House
Hospital/Clinic
Temple
Church
House Church
Military Base
Mosque
School
Market

Learners tend to make better maps when they...

- Do a rough draft first and copy it to a clean sheet of paper afterwards.
- Get new ideas by walking around and seeing what others are doing on their maps.
- Understand they will be presenting the map to the group at the end of the training.
- Use crayons or color pencils to make the map more colorful.

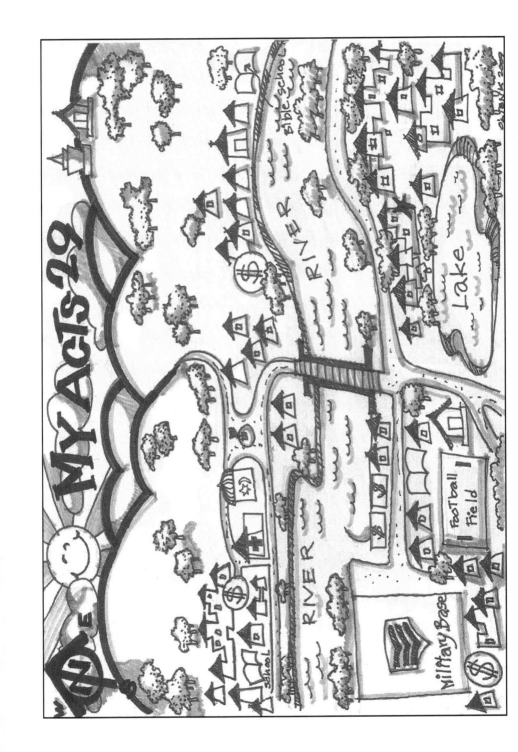

6

Walk

Walk introduces learners to Jesus as a Son: a son/daughter honors his/her father, desires unity, and wants the family to succeed. The Father called Jesus "beloved" and the Holy Spirit descended upon Jesus at His baptism. Jesus was successful in His ministry because He depended on the power of the Holy Spirit.

In the same way, we must depend on the power of the Holy Spirit in our lives. We have four commands to obey concerning the Holy Spirit: walk with the Spirit, do not grieve the Spirit, be filled with the Spirit, and do not quench the Spirit. Jesus is with us today and wants to help us even as He helped people on the roads of Galilee. We can call to Jesus if we need healing from something that is stopping us from following Him.

Worship

- Ask someone to pray for God's presence and blessing.
- Sing two choruses or hymns together.

PRAYER

- Arrange learners into pairs with someone they have not been a partner with before.
- Each learner shares with their partner the answer to the following questions:

    1. How can we pray for lost people you know to be saved?
    2. How can we pray for the group you are training?

- If a partner has not started training anyone, pray for potential people in their sphere of influence they can begin to train.
- Partners pray together.

STUDY

Out of Gas ❧

"What would you think if I pushed my motorcycle everywhere and never filled it up with gas?"

- Ask for a volunteer. The volunteer will be your "motorcycle." Push your motorcycle to work, to school, to the market, and to visit friends. At your friend's house, they ask to ride your "motorcycle" with you. Let them get on and then push them as well. Demonstrate how exhausting this would be.

"Obviously, it is much better when you put gasoline in your motorcycle. Then you can do all of these things much more easily."

- Turn the key and kick-start your "motorcycle." Make sure it makes a motorcycle noise.
- You may have to stop and "fix" the motorcycle several times, if it stops making noise. Do all the things you did previously, but now it is effortless because you do not have to push the motorcycle. When your friends ask to ride, let them get on the motorcycle, and say, "It's no problem. I have plenty of power now."

"The motorcycle is like our spiritual life. Many people 'push' their spiritual life around, relying on their own strength. As a result, their Christian walk is difficult, and they want to give up. Others have discovered the power of the Holy Spirit in their life. He is like gas in the motorcycle. The Holy Spirit gives us the power we need to do whatever Jesus commands."

Review

Each review session is the same. Ask learners to stand and recite previous lessons learned. Make sure they do the hand motions, too.

What Are Eight Pictures That Help Us Follow Jesus?
Soldier, Seeker, Shepherd, Sower, Son, Saint, Servant, Steward

Multiply
What are three things a steward does?
What was God's first command to man?
What was Jesus' last command to man?
How can I be fruitful and multiply?
What are the two seas located in Israel?
Why are they so different?
Which one do you want to be like?

Love

What are three things a shepherd does?

What is the most important command to teach others?

Where does love come from?

What is simple worship?

Why do we have simple worship?

How many people does it take to have simple worship?

Pray

What are three things a saint does?

How should we pray?

How will God answer us?

What is God's phone number?

Obey

What are three things a servant does?

Who has the highest authority?

What are four commands Jesus has given to every believer?

How should we obey Jesus?

What did Jesus promise us?

What is Jesus Like?

> *—Matthew 3:16, 17—After Jesus was baptized, He went up immediately from the water. The heavens suddenly opened for Him, and He saw the Spirit of God descending like a dove and coming down on Him. And there came a voice from heaven: "This is My beloved Son. I take delight in Him!" (HCSB)*

"Jesus is a Son. 'Son of Man' was Jesus' favorite description for Himself. He was the first to call the eternal God, 'Father.' Because of His resurrection, now we can be a part of God's family, too."

Son/Daughter
 Move hands towards mouth as if you are eating. Sons eat a lot!

What are Three Things a Son Does?

—John 17:4, 18-21—(Jesus says...) I brought glory to you here on earth by completing the work you gave me to do.

Just as you sent me into the world, I am sending them into the world. And I give myself as a holy sacrifice for them so they can be made holy by your truth. I am praying not only for these disciples but also for all who will ever believe in me through their message. I pray that they will all be one, just as you and I are one—as you are in me, Father, and I am in you. And may they be in us so that the world will believe you sent me. (NLT)

1. Sons honor their father.

   Jesus brought glory to His Father while He was on earth.

2. Sons want unity in the family.

   Jesus wants His followers to be one, just as He and His father are one.

3. Sons want the family to succeed.

   Just as God sent Jesus to the world to succeed, Jesus sends us to succeed as well.

"Jesus is a son, and He lives in us. As we follow Him, we will be sons and daughters. We will honor our Heavenly

Father, desire unity in the family of God, and work toward the success of God's Kingdom."

Why Was Jesus' Ministry Successful?

—Luke 4:14—(after His temptation) And Jesus returned to Galilee in the power of the Spirit, and news about Him spread through all the surrounding district. (NASB)

"The Holy Spirit gave Jesus the power to succeed. Jesus ministered in the power of the Spirit, not by His own strength. When we follow Jesus, we copy the way He ministered. Jesus continually depended on the Holy Spirit. Since Jesus had to depend on the Holy Spirit, how much more should we!"

What Did Jesus Promise Believers About the Holy Spirit Before the Cross?

—John 14:16-18—And I will ask the Father, and he will give you another Counselor to be with you forever—the Spirit of truth. The world cannot accept him, because it neither sees him nor knows him. But you know him, for he lives with you and will be in you. I will not leave you as orphans; I will come to you.

1. He will give us the Holy Spirit.
2. The Holy Spirit will be with us forever.
3. The Holy Spirit will be in us.
4. We will always be a part of God's family.

"We are a part of His family because the Holy Spirit lives in us."

What Did Jesus Promise Believers About the Holy Spirit After His Resurrection?

> —*Acts 1:8—But you will receive power when the Holy Spirit comes on you. And you will be my witnesses in Jerusalem, and in all Judea and Samaria, and to the ends of the earth. (NLT)*

"The Holy Spirit will give us power when He comes on us."

What Are Four Commands to Obey Concerning the Holy Spirit?

> —*Galatians 5:16—But I say, walk by the Spirit, and you will not carry out the desire of the flesh.(NASB)*

WALK BY THE SPIRIT

- Choose a volunteer. Partners should be men/men or women/women and not mixed. (Do it this way unless it is culturally appropriate for men and women to perform skits together.)

  "My partner and I are going to show you some truths about walking with God's Spirit. In this skit, I am myself, and my partner is the Holy Spirit. The Bible says, 'Walk by the Spirit.'"

- Demonstrate "walking by the Spirit" with your partner. You and your partner walk together hand in hand, shoulder to shoulder and talk together. When the Holy Spirit wants to go somewhere, go with him/her. Sometimes, though, try to walk away from where the Holy Spirit is going. Stay joined with your partner because the Holy Spirit never leaves us. Struggle because he is going one way, and you are going another.

"We should walk the path the Holy Spirit desires and not our own. Sometimes we want to go our own direction, and this causes spiritual problems and great conflict in our heart."

> **Walk by the Spirit**
> "Walk" the fingers on both hands.

⊕

—Ephesians 4:30—And don't grieve God's Holy Spirit, who sealed you for the day of redemption. (HCSB)

DO NOT GRIEVE THE SPIRIT

"The Bible says, 'Do not grieve the Holy Spirit.' The Holy Spirit has feelings, and we can make Him sad."

- Walk around with the Holy Spirit (your partner) and start gossiping about someone in the group. When you do this, the Holy Spirit begins to grieve. Pretend to pick a fight with another learner, and the Holy Spirit grieves again.

"Be careful how you live your life, because the Holy Spirit is in you and can be grieved. We can make the Holy Spirit sad by what we do or say."

> **Do not grieve the Spirit.**
> Rub eyes like you are crying then shake head signaling "no."

—Ephesians 5:18—Don't be drunk with wine, because that will ruin your life. Instead, be filled with the Holy Spirit… (NLT)

BE FILLED WITH THE SPIRIT

"The Bible says, 'Be filled with the Spirit.' This means that we need the Spirit in every part of our lives and every part of the day.

When we received Christ, we received all of the Holy Spirit we will ever have on earth. It is not possible to get 'more' of the Holy Spirit. However, it is possible for the Holy Spirit to get 'more' of us! We choose each day how much of our lives He will fill. This command is for Him to fill every part of our lives."

Be filled with the Spirit.
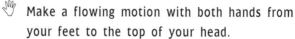 Make a flowing motion with both hands from your feet to the top of your head.

—I Thessalonians 5:19—Do not quench the Spirit. (NASB)

DO NOT QUENCH THE SPIRIT

"The Bible says, 'Do not quench the Spirit.' This means that we should not try to stop His work in our lives."

- Walk around with the Holy Spirit (your partner) and tell the group that the Holy Spirit wants you to witness to one of the learners. Refuse to witness, give an excuse, and move along your way. The Holy Spirit asks you to pray for a sick person, but you refuse, give an excuse, and go a different direction.

"We often hinder God's work by giving excuses and doing what we want instead of following the Holy Spirit's leading. We can quench the Holy Spirit by what we do not do or do not say. It is as if we are trying to put out the fire of the Holy Spirit in our lives."

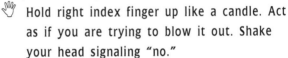

Do not quench the Spirit.
Hold right index finger up like a candle. Act as if you are trying to blow it out. Shake your head signaling "no."

Memory Verse

–John 7:38–Anyone who believes in me may come and drink! For the Scriptures declare, "Rivers of living water will flow from his heart." (NLT)

- Everyone stands and says the memory verse ten times together. The first six times, learners use their Bible or student notes. The last four times, they say the verse from memory. Learners should say the reference before each time they quote the verse and sit down when finished.
- This will help the trainers know who has finished the lesson in the "Practice" section.

PRACTICE

- Ask learners to sit facing their prayer partner for this session. Partners take turns teaching each other the lesson.

  "The person *who lives the farthest away from the meeting place* in the pair will be the leader."

- Follow the *Training Trainers Process* on page 9.
- Emphasize how you want them to teach everything in the "Study" section exactly the way you did.

  "Ask the questions, read the Scriptures together, and answer the questions the same way that I did with you."

- After the learners have practiced training each other the lesson, ask learners to think about someone that they will share this lesson with outside the training.

  "Take a few moments to think about someone you can teach this lesson to outside of this training. Write that person's name at the top of the first page of this lesson."

ENDING

This is a meaningful time of ministry. If you are running short on time, you might put this section at the beginning of the next lesson or do it another time. You might also use this section if your group wants to have a devotional time during the evening in a seminar setting.

Jesus Is Here ❧

—Hebrews 13:8—Jesus Christ never changes! He is the same yesterday, today, and forever. (CEV)

—Matthew 15:30-31—And large crowds came to Him, bringing with them those who were lame, crippled, blind, mute, and many others, and they laid them down at His feet; and He healed them. So the crowd marveled as they saw the mute speaking, the crippled restored, and the lame walking, and the blind seeing; and they glorified the God of Israel. (NASB)

—John 10:10—The thief comes only to steal and kill and destroy; I have come that they may have life, and have it to the full.

"In Hebrews 13:8, the Bible says that Jesus is the same yesterday, today, and forever.

In Matthew 15:30, the Bible says that Jesus healed many people with many different problems.

In John 10:10, the Bible says that Satan comes to kill, steal, and destroy, but Jesus came to give us abundant life.

In fact, we know that Jesus is here with us right now. If there is an area in your life that needs healing, He wants to heal it now even as He did in Matthew 15. Satan wants to kill you and steal from you; Jesus wants to give you abundant life.

Maybe you can relate spiritually to someone in the Matthew 15:30 passage. Is your walk with Jesus strong, or has Satan made you lame?"

🖐 Limp around.

"Jesus is here. Ask Him, and He will heal you so you can walk with Him again.

Can you see where God is working, or has Satan blinded your eyes with discouragement?"

🖐 Cover your eyes.

"Jesus is here. Ask Him, and He will heal you so you can see where He is working again.

Are you sharing the good news of Jesus with all those around you, or are you mute?"

🖐 Cover your mouth.

"Jesus is here. Ask Him, and He will heal you so you can speak about Him with boldness again.

Are you helping others, or has Satan hurt you to the point you can't give anymore?"

🖐 Carry your arm as if it is hurt and in a sling.

"Jesus is here. Ask Him, and He will heal you so you can put the past behind you and walk with Him again.

Do you have some problem in your life that is keeping you from following Jesus with your whole heart?

Whatever your affliction, Jesus is here now and can heal you. Call out to Jesus, let Him heal you, and bring great glory to God!"

- Ask partners to pray for each other, asking Jesus to heal them from anything keeping them from following Him with all their heart.

7

Go

Go introduces Jesus as a Seeker: seekers search for new places, lost people, and new opportunities. How did Jesus decide where to go and minister? He did not do it Himself; He looked to see where God was working; He joined God; and He knew that God loved Him and would show Him. How should we decide where to minister?–the same way that Jesus did.

Where is God working? He is working among the poor, captives, sick, and oppressed. Another place God is working is in our families. He wants to save our entire family. Learners locate people and places where God is working on their Acts 29 Map.

WORSHIP

- Ask someone to pray for God's presence and blessing.
- Sing two choruses or hymns together.

PRAYER

- Arrange learners into pairs with someone they have not been a partner with before.
- Each learner shares with their partner the answer to the following questions:

  1. How can we pray for lost people you know to be saved?
  2. How can we pray for the group you are training?

- If a partner has not started training anyone, pray for potential people in their sphere of influence they can begin to train.
- Partners pray together.

STUDY

Review

Each review session is the same. Ask learners to stand and recite previous lessons learned. Make sure they do the hand motions, too.

What Are Eight Pictures That Help Us Follow Jesus?
Soldier, Seeker, Shepherd, Sower, Son, Saint, Servant, Steward

Love
What are three things a shepherd does?
What is the most important command to teach others?
Where does love come from?
What is simple worship?
Why do we have simple worship?
How many people does it take to have simple worship?

Pray

What are three things a saint does?

How should we pray?

How will God answer us?

What is God's phone number?

Obey

What are three things a servant does?

Who has the highest authority?

What are four commands Jesus has given to every believer?

How should we obey Jesus?

What is a promise Jesus has given to every believer?

Walk

What are three things a son does?

What was the source of power in Jesus' ministry?

What did Jesus promise believers about the Holy Spirit before the cross?

What did Jesus promise believers about the Holy Spirit after His resurrection?

What are four commands to follow about the Holy Spirit?

What is Jesus Like?

—Luke 19:10—For the Son of Man has come to seek and to save that which was lost. (NASB)

"Jesus is a Seeker. He sought lost people. He also sought God's will and God's kingdom first in His life."

Seeker

Look back and forth with hand above eyes.

What are Three Things a Seeker Does?

—Mark 1:37, 38—And when they found him, they exclaimed: "Everyone is looking for you!" Jesus replied, "Let us go somewhere else—to the nearby villages—so I can preach there also. That is why I have come."

1. Seekers like to find new places.
2. Seekers like to find lost people.
3. Seekers like to find new opportunities.

"Jesus is a seeker and lives in us. As we follow Him, we will be seekers, too."

How Did Jesus Decide Where To Minister?

—John 5:19, 20—Jesus gave them this answer: "I tell you the truth, the Son can do nothing by himself; he can do only what he sees his Father doing, because whatever the Father does the Son also does. For the Father loves the Son and shows him all he does. Yes, to your amazement he will show him even greater things than these."

"Jesus said, 'I do nothing by myself.'"

🖐 Put one hand over heart and shake head 'no'.

"Jesus said, 'I look to see where God is working.'"

🖐 Put one hand over eyes; search left and right.

"Jesus said, 'Where He is working, I join Him.'"

✋ Point hand towards a place in front of you and shake head yes.

"Jesus said, 'And I know He loves me and will show me.'"

✋ Raise hands upwards in praise and then cross them over your heart.

How Should We Decide Where To Minister?

—I John 2:5, 6—But those who obey God's word truly show how completely they love him. That is how we know we are living in him. Those who say they live in God should live their lives as Jesus did. (NLT)

"We decide where to minister the same way Jesus did:

I do nothing by myself."

✋ Put one hand over heart and shake head 'no'.

"I look to see where God is working."

✋ Put one hand over eyes; search left and right.

"Where He is working, I join Him."

✋ Point hand towards a place in front of you and shake head yes.

"And I know He loves me and will show me."

✋ Raise hands upwards in praise and then cross them over your heart.

117

How can we know if God is working?

–John 6:44–No one can come to Me unless the Father who sent Me draws him, and I will raise him up on the last day.

"If someone is interested in learning more about Jesus, then you know God is working. John 6:44 says that only God can bring people to Himself. We ask questions, sow spiritual seeds, and see if there is a response. If they respond, we know that God is working."

Where is Jesus Working?

–Luke 4:18-19–The Spirit of the Lord is upon me, because he anointed me to preach the gospel to the poor. He has sent me to proclaim release to the captives, and recovery of sight to the blind, to set free those who are oppressed, to proclaim the favorable year of the Lord. (NASB)

1. The poor
2. The captives
3. The sick
4. The oppressed

"Jesus ministered and ministers to these kinds of people. It is important to remember; however, that He did not minister to every poor person, or every oppressed person. In our own effort, we want to help everyone. Jesus looked to see where the Father was working and joined Him. We need to do the same. If we try to minister to every oppressed person, it is a sure sign we are trying to do it all ourselves."

Where is Another Place that Jesus is working?

"Did you know that God loves your whole family? It is His will that they all are saved and spend eternity together with Him. There are many examples in the Bible when God saved a whole family."

Demon-Possessed Man–Mark 5

"The demon-possessed man was radically changed. He wanted to go with Jesus, but Jesus asked him to return to his family and tell them what had happened. Many people in the surrounding villages were amazed at what Jesus had done. When God saves one person, He wants to save many others around them."

Cornelius–Acts 10

"God told Peter to go speak with Cornelius. When Peter spoke, the Holy Spirit filled Cornelius and all who heard the message. Cornelius believed, and all those around him believed as well."

Jailer at Philippi–Acts 16

"Paul and Silas remained in the jail even though an earthquake caused the prison doors to open. The jailer was amazed at this and believed on the Lord Jesus. God saved his whole household, as well.

Never give up believing and praying that everyone in your family will be saved and spend eternity together!"

Memory Verse

—John 12:26—Anyone who wants to be my disciple must follow me, because my servants must be where I am. And the Father will honor anyone who serves me. (NLT)

- Everyone stands and says the memory verse ten times together. The first six times, learners use their Bible or student notes. The last four times, they say the verse from memory. Learners should say the verse reference before each time they quote the verse and sit down when finished.
- This will help the trainers know who has finished the lesson in the "Practice" section.

PRACTICE

- Ask learners to sit facing their prayer partner for this session. Partners take turns teaching each other the lesson.

  "The person *with the most brothers and sisters* in the pair is the leader."

- Follow the *Training Trainers Process* on page 9.
- Emphasize that you want them to teach everything in the "Study" section exactly the way you did.

  "Ask the questions, read the Scriptures together, and answer the questions the same way that I did with you."

- After the learners have practiced training each other the lesson, ask learners to think about someone that they will share this lesson with outside the training.

"Take a few moments to think about someone you can teach this lesson to outside of this training. Write that person's name at the top of the first page of this lesson."

ENDING

ACTS 29 MAP - Part 2 ☙

"On your Acts 29 Map, draw and label places where Jesus is working. Identify at least five places on your map where you know Jesus is working and draw a cross at each place. Label how God is working in that area."

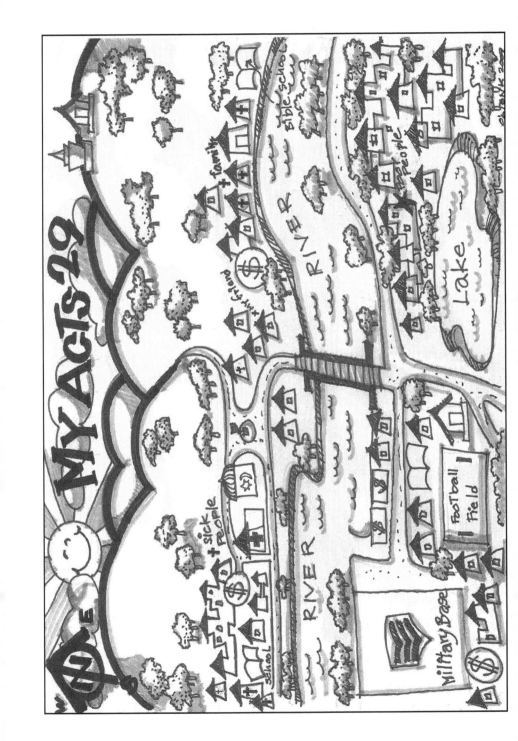

8

Share

Share introduces Jesus as a Soldier: soldiers fight enemies, endure hardship, and set the captives free. Jesus is a soldier; when we follow Him, we will be soldiers, too.

As soon as we join God where He is working, we encounter spiritual warfare. How do believers defeat Satan? We defeat him by Jesus' death on the cross, sharing our testimony, and not being afraid to die for our faith.

A powerful testimony would be if I share the story of my life before I met Jesus, then how I met Jesus, and the difference that walking with Jesus is making in my life. Testimonies are more effective when we limit our sharing to three or four minutes, when we don't share our conversion age (because age doesn't matter), and when we use language unbelievers can understand easily.

The session ends with a contest: who can most quickly write the names of 40 lost people they know. Prizes are given for first, second, and third place, but ultimately everyone gets a prize because we are all "winners" when we know how to give our testimony.

WORSHIP

- Ask someone to pray for God's presence and blessing.
- Sing two choruses or hymns together.

PRAYER

- Arrange learners into pairs with someone they have not been a partner with before.
- Each learner shares with their partner the answer to the following questions:

    1. How can we pray for lost people you know to be saved?
    2. How can we pray for the group you are training?

- If a partner has not started training anyone, pray for potential people in their sphere of influence they can begin to train.
- Partners pray together.

STUDY

Review

Each review session is the same. Ask learners to stand and recite previous lessons learned. Make sure they do the hand motions, too.

What Are Eight Pictures That Help Us Follow Jesus?
Soldier, Seeker, Shepherd, Sower, Son, Saint, Servant, Steward

Pray

What are three things a saint does?
How should we pray?
How will God answer us?
What is God's phone number?

Obey

What are three things a servant does?
Who has the highest authority?
What are four commands Jesus has given to every believer?
How should we obey Jesus?
What is a promise Jesus has given to every believer?

Walk

What are three things a son does?
What was the source of power in Jesus' ministry?
What did Jesus promise believers about the Holy Spirit before the cross?
What did Jesus promise believers about the Holy Spirit after His resurrection?
What are four commands to follow about the Holy Spirit?

Go

What are three things a seeker does?
How did Jesus decide where to minister?
How should we decide where to minister?
Where is Jesus working?
Where is another place Jesus is working?

What is Jesus Like?

—Matthew 26:53—Don't you know that I could ask my Father, and right away he would send me more than twelve armies of angels? (CEV)

"Jesus is a Soldier. He could call 12 armies of angels to His defense because He is the Commander in Chief of God's army. He engaged Satan in spiritual warfare and ultimately defeated the evil one on the cross."

Soldier
✋ Raise sword.

What are Three Things a Soldier Does?

—Mark 1:12-15—Right away God's Spirit made Jesus go into the desert. He stayed there for forty days while Satan tested him. Jesus was with the wild animals, but angels took care of him. After John was arrested, Jesus went to Galilee and told the good news that comes from God. He said, "The time has come! God's kingdom will soon be here. Turn back to God and believe the good news!" (CEV)

1. Soldiers fight enemies.

"Jesus battled the enemy and won."

2. Soldiers suffer hardship.

"Jesus suffered many things while He was on Earth."

3. Soldiers set the captives free.

"Jesus' kingdom was coming to set people free."

"Jesus is a soldier. He commands God's army and engages Satan in spiritual warfare. Jesus has won the victory for us on the cross. As Jesus lives in us, we will be victorious soldiers as well. We will fight spiritual warfare, suffer hardship to please our Commander, and help set the captives free."

How Do We Defeat Satan?

—Revelation 12:11—And they have defeated him by the blood of the Lamb and by their testimony. And they did not love their lives so much that they were afraid to die. (NLT)

BY THE BLOOD OF THE LAMB

"We overcome Satan because of the blood Jesus shed on the cross. We are more than conquerors through Him and what He has done."

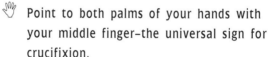

Blood of the Lamb
Point to both palms of your hands with your middle finger–the universal sign for crucifixion.

"As you encounter spiritual warfare, remember that Jesus has defeated Satan on the cross! Satan shakes, snivels, and cries anytime he sees Jesus. He starts begging Jesus not to hurt him and to leave him alone.

The good news is that Jesus lives in us. Therefore, whenever Satan sees Jesus in us, Satan starts to shake and snivel. He cries like a baby! Satan is a defeated foe because of what Jesus did on the cross! Never forget this:

no matter how difficult things are, we will win! We will win! We will win!"

BY OUR TESTIMONY

"We overcome Satan by the powerful weapon of our testimony. No one can argue with our testimony of what Jesus has done in our lives. We can use this weapon at any time and any place."

Testimony
Cup hands around mouth as if you are speaking to someone.

BY BEING NOT AFRAID TO DIE

"Our eternity with God is secure. To be with Him is better; to be here is necessary to spread the Gospel. We can't lose!"

Not afraid to die
Place wrists together, as if in chains.

What Is a Powerful Testimony Outline?

MY LIFE BEFORE I MET JESUS

Before
Point to the left side in front of you.

"Describe what your life was like before you became a believer. If you grew up in a Christian home, unbelievers find it interesting to hear what a Christian home is like."

HOW I MET JESUS

How

✋ Point to the center in front of you.

"Describe how you came to believe in and follow Jesus."

MY LIFE SINCE I MET JESUS

✋ Turn to your right and move hands up and down.

"Describe what it has been like to follow Jesus since your conversion and what your relationship with him means to you."

ASK A SIMPLE QUESTION

"At the end of your testimony, ask the person, 'Would you like to hear more about following Jesus?' This is the, 'Is God working?' question."

✋ Point to your temple—as if you are thinking about a question.

"If they say 'yes,' you know that God is working in this situation. God is the only one who draws people to Himself. At that point, share more with them about following Jesus.

If they say 'no,' God is not working in this situation now. Ask them if you can pray a prayer of blessing for them, do so, and continue on your way."

What Are Some Important Guidelines To Follow?

LIMIT YOUR INITIAL TESTIMONY TO THREE OR FOUR MINUTES

"There are many lost people in this world; limiting your initial testimony helps to see who is responsive and who is not. Above all, follow the leading of the Holy Spirit. New believers feel more comfortable with the idea of only sharing three or four *minutes* and not three or four *hours*!"

DON'T TELL THE AGE YOU WERE WHEN YOU BECAME A BELIEVER

"Your age when you became a follower of Jesus does not matter, but it can send the wrong message to an unbeliever when you share your testimony. If they are younger than you were when you became a believer, they might think they can wait until later. If they are older than you were when you became a believer, they might think they have missed their chance. The Bible says *today* is the day of salvation. Telling your age at conversion usually only confuses the situation."

DON'T USE CHRISTIAN LANGUAGE

"After people have become believers for even a short time, they begin to pick up language that other Christians use. Phrases, like 'washed in the blood of the lamb' or 'walked down the aisle' or 'I talked to the preacher,' sound like a foreign language to unbelievers. We use as little Christian language as possible, so those we share our testimony with can understand the Gospel as clearly as possible."

Memory Verse

> *—1Corinthians 15:3,4—For what I received I passed on to you as of first importance: that Christ died for our sins according to the Scriptures, that he was buried, that he was raised on the third day according to the Scriptures...*

- Everyone stands and says the memory verse ten times together. The first six times, learners use their Bible or student notes. The last four times, they say the verse from memory. Learners should say the reference of the verse at the beginning of the verse and sit down when finished.
- This will help the trainers know who has finished the lesson in the "Practice" section.

PRACTICE

- Announce to learners that you want them to write their testimony down in their notebooks using the outline you have given them. Tell them they will have 10 minutes to do this, and then you are going to call on someone in the group to give their testimony.

- At the end of 10 minutes, ask the learners to put their pens down. Tell them you are going to call on someone to give their testimony to the group. Pause a few seconds. Then, announce that you are going to give your testimony to the group. There will be a great sigh of relief!

- Share your testimony using the outline and guidelines above. At the end of your testimony, go step-by-step through the outline and guidelines, asking learners if you gave your testimony correctly.

- During the "Practice" part of this lesson, you will use a watch to time the learners. Have learners break into pairs and tell them they will have three minutes each to share their testimony.

  "The *loudest* person will be the leader, the person who goes first."

- Time the first person in the pair and say, "stop" at the three-minute mark. Ask learners if their partner followed the outline and used the four guidelines for a powerful testimony. Then, ask the second person in the pair to share their testimony for three minutes. Again, ask learners for feedback.

- When both partners have shared, direct learners to find a new partner, determine who has the loudest voice, and practice sharing their testimony again. Try to divide the group into pairs at least four times.

- After teaching each other the lesson, ask learners to think of someone with whom they will share this lesson after the training. Have them write the person's name at the top of the first page of the lesson.

Salt and Sugar ∞

Use this illustration during one of the feedback times to emphasize how important it is to share from the heart.

"Fresh, ripe fruit is always so tasty! It is sweet and fills your mouth with joy! When I think about pineapple, yellow and sweet, it makes my mouth water.

I know a way you can make fruit taste even better, though! Add a little sugar, salt, or peppers. Uhhhmmm! Then it is really delicious! I can just taste it now!

In the same way, whenever you teach a lesson or share the Gospel, God's word is always good, just like the fruit. We should taste and see that the Lord is good. However, when you share from your heart with emotion, it is like adding sugar, salt, or peppers to the fruit. It makes it especially delicious!

So, when you are sharing with your partner this next time, I want you to add plenty of salt, sugar or pepper to what you say."

ENDING

Who Can List Forty Lost People the Fastest? ○？

- Ask each person to take out their notebook and number from one to 40.

"We are going to have a contest. We will be giving prizes for first, second, and third places."

- Tell everyone that when you say, "Go!" they are to write down the names of 40 unbelievers they know. If they cannot remember their names, they can write something like "the barber" or "the postman." Make sure no one starts before you say go.
- Some will be tempted to start when you give the directions. It helps to have learners raise their pens in the air while you are giving the instructions.
- Launch the contest and have people stand when they have finished their list. Give prizes to first, second, and third place. "There are two reasons believers give that they can't share their faith: they do not know how, and they do not know with whom to share the Gospel. In this lesson, we have solved both problems. You now know how to share the Gospel and have a list of people with whom to share."

- Ask learners to put a star beside five people on their list with whom they will share their testimony. Encourage them to do so during the next week.

"Look at your hand. Your five fingers can remind you of five lost people you can pray for every day. When you are washing dishes, writing, or typing on the computer, let the five fingers on your hand remind you to pray."

- Ask learners to spend time praying aloud as a group for the lost people on their list.
- After the prayer time, give everyone a piece of candy as a prize, saying, "We are all winners now because we know how to share the Gospel and who to share with in our lives."

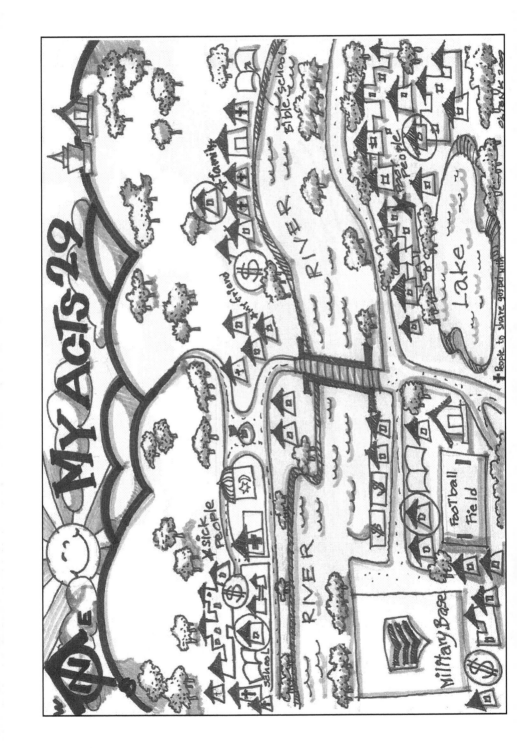

9

Sow

Sow introduces Jesus as a Sower: sowers plant seeds, tend their fields, and rejoice in a great harvest. Jesus is a Sower and He lives in us; when we follow Him, we will be sowers as well. When we sow a little, we reap a little. When we sow much, we reap much.

What should we sow into people's lives? Only the simple gospel can transform them and bring them back to God's family. Once we know that God is working in a person's life, we share the simple gospel with them. We know it is the power of God to save them.

WORSHIP

- Ask someone to pray for God's presence and blessing.
- Sing two choruses or hymns together.

PRAYER

- Arrange learners into pairs with someone they have not been a partner with before.
- Each learner shares with their partner the answer to the following questions:

    1. How can we pray for lost people you know to be saved?
    2. How can we pray for the group you are training?

- If a partner has not started training anyone, pray for potential people in their sphere of influence they can begin to train.
- Partners pray together.

STUDY

Review

Each review session is the same. Ask learners to stand and recite previous lessons learned. Make sure they do the hand motions, too.

What Are Eight Pictures That Help Us Follow Jesus?
Soldier, Seeker, Shepherd, Sower, Son, Saint, Servant, Steward

Obey
What are three things a servant does?
Who has the highest authority?
What are four commands Jesus has given to every believer?
How should we obey Jesus?
What is a promise Jesus has given to every believer?

Walk

What are three things a son does?

What was the source of power in Jesus' ministry?

What did Jesus promise believers about the Holy Spirit before the cross?

What did Jesus promise believers about the Holy Spirit after His resurrection?

What are four commands to follow about the Holy Spirit?

Go

What are three things a seeker does?

How did Jesus decide where to minister?

How should we decide where to minister?

Where is Jesus working?

Where is another place Jesus is working?

Share

What are three things a soldier does?

How do we overcome Satan?

What is a powerful testimony outline?

What are some important guidelines to follow?

What is Jesus Like?

—Matthew 13:36, 37—Then He (Jesus) left the crowds and went into the house and His disciples came to Him and said, "Explain to us the parable of the tares of the field." And He said, "The one who sows the good seed is the Son of Man..." (NASB)

"Jesus is a Sower and Lord of the harvest."

Sower

Scatter seed with hand.

What are Three Things a Sower Does?

—Mark 4:26-29—Again Jesus said: God's kingdom is like what happens when a farmer scatters seed in a field. The farmer sleeps at night and is up and around during the day. Yet the seeds keep sprouting and growing, and he does not understand how. It is the ground that makes the seeds sprout and grow into plants that produce grain. Then when harvest season comes and the grain is ripe, the farmer cuts it with a sickle.(CEV)

1. Sowers plant good seed.
2. Sowers tend their field.
3. Sowers expect a harvest

"Jesus is a Sower and lives in us. He plants good seed in our hearts, while Satan wants to plant bad seed. The seed that Jesus plants leads to eternal life. When we follow Him, we will be sowers as well. We will plant the good seed of the Gospel. We will tend the field where God has sent us, and we will expect a great harvest."

What is the Simple Gospel?

—Luke 24:1-7—On the first day of the week, very early in the morning, the women took the spices they had prepared and went to the tomb. They found the stone rolled away from the tomb, but when they entered, they did not find the body of the Lord Jesus. While they were wondering about this, suddenly two men in clothes that gleamed like lightning stood beside them. In their fright the women bowed down with their faces to the ground, but the men said to them, "Why do you look for the living among the dead? He is not here; he has risen! Remember how he told you, while

he was still with you in Galilee: 'The Son of Man must be delivered over to the hands of sinners, be crucified and on the third day be raised again.'"

FIRST...

"God created a perfect world."

✋ Make a large circle with your hands.

"He made man a part of his family."

✋ Clasp hands together.

SECOND...

"Man disobeyed God and brought sin and suffering into the world."

✋ Raise fists and pretend to fight.

"So man had to leave God's family."

✋ Clasp hands together and then pull them far apart.

THIRD...

"God sent His Son Jesus to earth. He lived a perfect life."

✋ Raise hands above head and make a downward motion.

"Jesus died on the cross for our sins."

🖐 Put the middle finger of each hand in the palm of the other.

"He was buried."

🖐 Hold right elbow with left hand and move right arm backward as if being buried.

"God raised Him to life on the third day."

🖐 Raise arm back up with three fingers.

"God saw Jesus' sacrifice for our sins and accepted it."

🖐 Put hands down with palms facing outward. Then, raise your hands and cross your heart.

FOURTH...

"Those who believe Jesus is God's son and has paid the price for their sins..."

🖐 Raise hands in worship.

"...repent of their sins..."

🖐 Palms are outward shielding the face; head turned away.

"...and ask to be saved..."

🖐 Cup hands.

"…are welcomed back to God's family."

🖐 **Clasp hands together.**

- Repeat the simple Gospel presentation several times with learners until they master the sequence. In our experience, most believers do not know how to share their faith, so take your time making sure everyone is clear about the meaning of the simple Gospel.
- Help learners master the sequence and hand motions by "building" the lesson. Start with the first point and repeat it several times. Then, share the second point and repeat it several times. Then, review the first point and the second point together several times. Afterwards, share the third point and repeat it several times. Then, do point one, point two, and point three together. Finally, teach the learners point four and review it several times. Learners should then be able to repeat the whole sequence with hand motions several times to demonstrate mastery.

Memory Verse

> *—Luke 8:15—But the seed on good soil stands for those with a noble and good heart, who hear the word, retain it, and by persevering produce a crop.*

- Everyone stands and says the memory verse ten times together. The first six times, learners use their Bible or student notes. The last four times, they say the verse from memory. Learners should say the verse reference before each time they quote the verse and sit down when finished.
- This will help the trainers know who has finished the lesson in the "Practice" section.

PRACTICE

- Ask learners to sit facing their prayer partner for this session. Partners take turns teaching each other the lesson.
- PLEASE READ! The practice portion of the sow lesson is different from the other practice times.
- Ask learners to stand facing their prayer partner. Both learners should repeat the simple Gospel together while performing the hand motions.
- When the first pairs finish, everyone should find another partner, face each other standing up, and say the simple Gospel with hand motions together.
- After the second pairs finish, learners should continue finding new partners until they have said the simple Gospel, with hand motions, with eight partners.
- When learners have finished with their eighth partner, ask everyone to say the simple Gospel with hand motions together as a group. You will be amazed how much better they can do this activity after they have practiced so many times!

REMEMBER TO PLANT THE GOSPEL SEED!

"Remember, plant the Gospel seed! If you do not plant the seed, there will be no harvest. If you plant only a few seeds, then you will have a small harvest. If you plant many seeds, then God will bless you with a great harvest. What kind of harvest do you want?

When you ask someone if they would like to know more about following Jesus and they say 'yes', then it is time to plant the Gospel seed. God is working in their life!

Sow the Gospel seed! No sowing = no harvest. Jesus is a Sower and He is looking for a large harvest.

Take a few moments to think about someone you can teach this lesson to outside of this training. Write that person's name at the top of the first page of this lesson."

Ending

Where is Acts 29:21? ca

"Turn in your Bibles to Acts 29:21."

- Learners will say there are only twenty-eight chapters in the book of Acts.

"My Bible has Acts 29."

- Have several learners come forward, point to the end of Chapter 28 in their Bibles and say they have Acts 29, as well.

"Now is 'Acts 29'. God is recording what the Holy Spirit is doing through us, and someday we will be able to read it. What do you want it to say? What is your vision? The map we have been working on is our 'Acts 29 Map' and vision for what God wants to do in our lives. I would like to share my Acts 29 Vision with you."

- Share your "Acts 29 Vision" with the group. Be sure to include the concept of two kinds of people: unbelievers and believers. God wants us to share the Gospel with unbelievers and train believers in how to follow Christ and share their faith.

"Our Acts 29 Maps represent the cross Jesus has called us to carry. Now we want to enter a holy time of presenting our maps, praying for one another, and committing our lives to follow Jesus."

ACTS 29 MAP - Part 3 ∞

- Tell learners to mark possible new group sites on their map. Ask learners to mark at least three possible locations for new disciple groups on their maps. They should write the name of the area, possible group leader, and host beside the group.
- If they have already started a group, celebrate and have them put it on the map. If they have not started a group yet, help them discern where God is working.
- This is the last time learners have to prepare their maps before they present them. Allow extra time as needed.

10

Take Up

Take Up is the closing session for the seminar. Jesus gave us the command to take up our cross and follow Him every day. The Acts 29 Map is a picture of the cross that Jesus has called each learner to carry.

In this final session, learners present their Acts 29 Map to the group. After each presentation, the group lays hands on the presenter and Acts 29 Map, praying for God's blessing and anointing on their ministry. The group then challenges the presenter by repeating the command, "Take up your cross, and follow Jesus," three times. Learners present their Acts 29 Map in turn until all have finished. The training time ends with a worship song of commitment to make disciples and a closing prayer by a recognized spiritual leader.

WORSHIP

- Ask someone to pray for God's presence and blessing.
- Sing two choruses or hymns together.

PRAYER

- Ask a recognized spiritual leader in the group to pray for God's blessing on this special time of commitment.

PRESENTATIONS

Review

Each review session is the same. Ask learners to stand and recite previous lessons learned. Make sure they do the hand motions, too.

What Are Eight Pictures That Help Us Follow Jesus?
Soldier, Seeker, Shepherd, Sower, Son, Saint, Servant, Steward

Multiply
What are three things a steward does?
What was God's first command to man?
What was Jesus' last command to man?
How can I be fruitful and multiply?
What are the two seas located in Israel?
Why are they so different?
Which one do you want to be like?

Love
What are three things a shepherd does?
What is the most important command to teach others?
Where does love come from?
What is simple worship?
Why do we have simple worship?
How many people does it take to have Simple Worship?

Pray

What are three things a saint does?

How should we pray?

How will God answer us?

What is God's phone number?

Obey

What are three things a servant does?

Who has the highest authority?

What are four commands Jesus has given to every believer?

How should we obey Jesus?

What is a promise Jesus has given to every believer?

Walk

What are three things a son does?

What was the source of power in Jesus' ministry?

What did Jesus promise believers about the Holy Spirit before the cross?

What did Jesus promise believers about the Holy Spirit after His resurrection?

What are four commands to follow about the Holy Spirit?

Go

What are three things a seeker does?

How did Jesus decide where to minister?

How should we decide where to minister?

Where is Jesus working?

Where is another place Jesus is working?

Share

What are three things a soldier does?

How do we overcome Satan?

What is a powerful testimony outline?

What are some important guidelines to follow?

Sow

What are three things a sower does?
What is the simple gospel we share?

What Does Jesus Command His Followers To Do Every Day?

> *—Luke 9:23—Then he said to them all: "If anyone would come after me, he must deny himself and take up his cross daily and follow me."*

"Deny yourself, take up your cross, and follow Jesus."

What Are Four Voices That Call Us To Take Up Our Cross?

THE VOICE ABOVE

> *—Mark 16:15—And then he told them, "Go into all the world and preach the Good News to everyone." (NLT)*

"Jesus calls us from Heaven to share the Gospel. He is the highest authority, and we should obey Him all of the time, immediately, and from a heart of love.

This is the voice from above."

Above
Point finger up towards the sky.

THE VOICE BELOW

> —*Luke 16:27-28*—*"Father," he said, "then I beg you to send him to my father's house—because I have five brothers— to warn them, so they won't also come to this place of torment." (HCSB)*

"Jesus told a story about a rich man who went to hell. In the story, the rich man wanted a poor man named Lazarus to leave Heaven and go to earth to warn his five brothers about the reality of hell. Abraham said that they had had enough warning. Lazarus could not go back to earth. People that have died and are now in hell call us to share the Gospel.

This is the voice from below."

Below

 Point finger down toward the ground.

THE VOICE INSIDE

> —*I Corinthians 9:16*—*Yet when I preach the gospel, I cannot boast, for I am compelled to preach. Woe to me if I do not preach the gospel!*

"The Holy Spirit within Paul compelled him to share the gospel. The same Holy Spirit calls us to take up our cross and share the Gospel.

This is the voice from inside."

Inside

 Point finger towards your heart.

THE VOICE OUTSIDE

—Acts 16:9—That night Paul had a vision: A man from Macedonia in northern Greece was standing there, pleading with him, "Come over to Macedonia and help us!" (NLT)

"Paul had planned to go into Asia, but the Holy Spirit wouldn't let him at that time. He had a vision that a man from Macedonia was pleading with him to come and preach the good news. Unreached peoples and groups around the world call us to take up our cross and share the Gospel.

This is the voice from outside."

Outside
Cup hand towards group and make a "come here" motion.

- Review the four voices with hand motions several times with learners asking them who the voice is, where it comes from, and what it says.

PRAYER

ACTS 29 MAPS

- Divide the learners into groups of about eight people each. Ask a recognized spiritual leader among participants in FJT to lead each group.
- Explain the following ministry time process to learners.
- Learners place their ACTS 29 Maps in the center of the circle and take turns presenting them to their group.

152

Afterwards, the group lays hands on the ACTS 29 Map and/or learner and prays for God's power and blessing on them.

- Everyone should pray aloud at the same time for the learner. The recognized leader of the group closes the time of prayer as the Spirit leads.

- At that point, the learner rolls up the map, puts it on his or her shoulder, and the group says, "Take up your cross and follow Jesus," three times in unison. Afterwards, the next learner presents their map and the process begins again.

- Before you begin, ask learners to repeat, "Take up your cross, and follow Jesus," three times, as they will do so after each person has presented their map. This will help everyone decide how to say the phrase in unison.

- When everyone in the group has presented their map, learners join another group that has not finished until all learners are in one large group that includes all seminar learners.

- End the training time singing a dedication worship song that is meaningful to learners in the group.

Part 3

REFERENCE

Further Study

Consult the following resources for a more in-depth discussion of the topic presented. In new areas of mission work, this is also a good list of first books to translate after the Bible.

Step 1: Grow Strong in the Lord

Bright, Bill (1971). *How to Be Filled with the Holy Spirit.* Campus Crusade for Christ.

Graham, Billy (1978). *The Holy Spirit: Activating God's Power in Your Life.* W Publishing Group.

Patterson, George and Scoggins, Richard (1994). *Church Multiplication Guide.* William Carey Library.

Hybels, Bill (1988). *Too Busy Not to Pray.* Intervarsity Press.

Murray, Andrew (2007). *With Christ in the School of Prayer.* Diggory Press.

Packer, J. I. (1993). *Knowing God.* Intervarsity Press.

Piper, John (2006). *What Jesus Demands from the World.* Crossway Books.

Step 2: Make Disciples

John Chen. *Training For Trainers (T4T)*. Unpublished, no date.

Blackaby, Henry T. and King, Claude V (1990). *Experiencing God: Knowing and Doing the Will of God.* Lifeway Press.

Billheimer, Paul (1975). *Destined for the Throne.* Christian Literature Crusade.

Carlton, R. Bruce (2003). *Acts 29: Practical Training in Facilitating Church-Planting Movements among the Neglected Harvest Fields.* Kairos Press.

Hodges, Herb (2001). *Tally Ho the Fox! The Foundation for Building World-Visionary, World Impacting, Reproducing Disciples.* Spiritual Life Ministries.

Neighbour, Ralph T (1967). *Witness, Take the Stand!* Unknown Binding.

Ogden, Greg (2003). *Transforming Discipleship: Making Disciples a Few at a Time.* Intervarsity Press.

Index

E

Earth 126
Empower 176
Example 32

F

Follow Jesus Training (FJT)
2, 3, 7, 11, 13, 15, 17, 18,
21, 22, 26, 28, 32, 33, 41,
152, 165, 168, 170, 172,
173, 174, 175, 177
Fruitful 54

G

Galilee 23, 49, 54, 55, 56,
57, 58, 99, 104, 126, 141
Gospel 7, 11, 18, 22, 35,
128, 131, 133, 134, 135,
140, 143, 144, 145, 150,
151, 152, 167, 171

H

Harvest 158
Heart 68
Heaven 49, 61, 89, 150,
151
Holy Spirit 22, 24, 25, 41,
47, 77, 90, 99, 101, 104,
105, 106, 107, 108, 115,
119, 125, 130, 139, 145,
149, 151, 152, 157, 168,
170

J

Jerusalem 25, 81, 105, 171

K

Kingdom 5, 7, 53, 80, 104

L

Learners 22, 29, 30, 31, 42,
49, 58, 63, 69, 73, 83, 94,
97, 108, 113, 120, 131,
143, 145, 147, 152, 169,
171, 172, 176
Lord 5, 7, 21, 22, 24, 25,
26, 36, 66, 68, 77, 81,
118, 119, 133, 139, 140,
157, 167

M

Map 176
Master 52
Memory 30, 58, 69, 83, 94,
108, 120, 131, 143
Ministry 4, 7, 104
Mission 4, 5, 6
Missionary 4, 5, 6, 174
Multiply 49, 54, 64, 75, 87,
101, 148, 163, 178

N

National 5, 13

T

Temple 13, 97
Testimony 128
Trainer 42

V

Vision 145

W

Walk 30, 99, 105, 106, 108,
    115, 125, 139, 149, 165,
    178
World 89, 157, 158, 163
Worship 34, 176, 178

Endnotes

1   Galen Currah and George Patterson, *Train and Multiply Workshop Manual* (Project World Outreach, 2004), p 28.

2   Currah and Patterson, p 17.

3   Currah and Patterson, pp 8, 9.

Appendix A

TRANSLATOR NOTES

The author gives permission to translate this training material into other languages as God directs. Please use the following guidelines when translating Follow Jesus Training materials (FJT):

- We recommend training others with FJT several times before starting the translation work. Translation should emphasize the meaning and not just be a literal, or word-for-word, translation. For example, if "Walk by the Spirit" is translated "Live by the Spirit" in your version of the Bible, use "Live by the Spirit," and modify hand motions as needed.
- The translation should be in the common language and not "religious language" of your people, as much as possible.
- Use a translation of the Bible that most of the people in your group will be able to understand. If there is only one translation and it is hard to understand, update terms in the Scriptures cited to make them clearer.
- Use a term that has a positive meaning for each of the eight pictures of Christ. Frequently, the training team may need to experiment with the "right term" several times before the correct one is found.
- Translate "Saint" as the term in your culture that conveys a holy person who worships, prays, and leads a high moral

life. If the word used to describe Jesus' holiness in your language is the same, it will not be necessary to use "Holy One." We use "Holy One" here because "Saint" does not appropriately describe Jesus.

- "Servant" can be difficult to translate in a positive sense, but it is very important that you do so. Be careful that the term you choose conveys a person who works hard, has a humble heart, and enjoys helping others. Most cultures have the idea of a "servant's heart."

- We developed all of the skits in Southeast Asia and generally fit that culture. Feel free to adapt them to your culture, being sure to use items and ideas familiar to your people.

- We would love to hear about your work and help in any way we can. Contact us at *translations@FollowJesusTraining. com* so we can collaborate and see more people follow Jesus!

Appendix B

FAQ

1. What is the main goal of *Making Radical Disciples*?

A small group of believers (who meet together for worship, prayer, Bible study, and hold each other accountable to follow Jesus' commands) is the basic building block of any healthy church or long-lasting movement. Our goal is to empower people to follow Jesus' strategy to reach the world by training them to do the first two steps in His strategy: grow strong in the Lord and share the Gospel. The missionary is sometimes the catalyst, but never the focus of a disciple-making-disciple movement.

In our experience, most believers have not experienced the transforming type of community that a disciple group creates. In a disciple-making-disciple movement, families disciple each other during family devotions; churches disciple their members in disciple groups and Sunday School classes; cell groups train their members how to disciple one another; and new church plants often start as small disciple groups. In a movement, disciple groups are anywhere and everywhere.

2. What is the difference between training and teaching?

Accountability. Teaching feeds the mind. Training feeds the hands and the heart. In a teaching setting, the teacher speaks a lot and the students ask a few questions. In a training setting, the learners speak a lot and the teacher asks a few questions. After teaching session, the usual question is "Did they like it?" After a training session, the key question is "Will they do it?"

3. What should I do if I can't finish the lesson in the time specified?

The training process is very important in FJT. Teach learners not only the content, but how to train others as well. Divide the "Study" sections in half if you don't have time to complete the whole lesson in one session. It is better to maintain the training process and split the lesson into two parts than leave out a part of the training process.

A common temptation is to skip the accountability and practice times, thus making the material more like a traditional Bible study. The key to multiplication, however, is accountability and practice. Do not skip these! Instead, divide the "Study" section over two meeting times and keep the training process intact.

4. Can you give me some ideas about how to start?

Start with yourself. You cannot give what you do not have. Learn the lessons and apply them to your life on a daily basis. Do not make the widespread mistake of thinking you have to reach some level before you start training others. It is also true that you cannot have what you do not give. If you are a believer, the Holy Spirit lives in you and thus guarantees you have reached the necessary level to begin training others.

While it is true that you cannot teach what you have not learned, it is also true that you cannot learn what you have not taught. Just do it. Go out and train others like a banshee. As you join God where He is working, there will be many opportunities to train others. Train five people with the same intensity that you would train fifty people and vice versa. Sow a little; reap a little. Sow much; reap much. The harvest you will see is most often in direct proportion to your commitment to train others.

5. What is the "Rule of 5?"

Learners must practice a lesson five times before they have the confidence necessary to train another person. The first time, the learners say, "That was such a good lesson. Thank you." The second time (after they have taught the lesson), they will say, "I think maybe I can teach this lesson, but I'm not sure." The third time, the learners say, "This lesson isn't as hard to teach as I thought. Maybe I can do it after all."

The fourth time, learners say, "I can see how important this lesson is and I want to teach others. It is getting easier each time." The fifth time, learners say, "I can train others to train others how to do this lesson. I am confident God will use this lesson to change the lives of my friends and family."

Practicing a lesson includes either "seeing" or "doing." For that reason, we recommend doing the practice time twice. Learners should practice once with their prayer partner and then switch to another partner and do the lesson again.

6. Why do you use so many hand motions?

It may seem childish at first, but most people soon realize that it helps them to memorize the material more quickly. Using hand motions aids those with kinesthetic and visual learning styles.

Be careful with the hand motions, however! Check the local customs of those you are training and make sure none of the hand motions are in poor taste or mean something different than you intend. We field tested the hand motions in this manual in several Southeast Asia countries, but checking ahead of time is still a good idea.

Don't be surprised if doctors, lawyers, and other more-educated learners enjoy learning and doing the hand motions. A comment we hear often is "Finally! Here are lessons I can teach others and they will understand and do them."

7. Why are the lessons so simple?

Jesus trained in a simple, memorable way. We use real-life examples (skits) and stories because that is what Jesus did. We believe a lesson is truly reproducible only if it can pass "the napkin test." (Can the lesson be written on a napkin over a casual meal and be immediately reproduced by the learner?) The lessons in FJT "teach themselves" and depend on the Holy Spirit to plant good seed. Simplicity is a key factor in reproducibility.

8. What are some common mistakes people make when they train others?

- *They Skip the Accountability Aspect of the Training:* The typical small group process is composed of worship, prayer, and Bible study. Training includes these three, but adds accountability. Most people believe they can't hold others accountable in a loving manner, so they skip this part. By setting an example and asking non-judgmental questions, however, a group can hold each other accountable and see significant spiritual growth.

- *They Talk Too Much:* In a typical ninety-minute session; the trainer may speak to the group a total of thirty minutes. Learners spend most of the time in a training session in joint worship, prayer, sharing, and practice. Many from a western educational background fall into the trap of reversing this time order.

- *They Focus On a Few and Not the Many:* The idea of one-on-one discipleship is good in theory, but falls short in practice. The Biblical norm seems to be making disciples in a small-group setting. Jesus spent the most time with Peter, James, and John. A group of men accompanied Peter on his disciple-making journeys and helped in the church at Jerusalem. Paul's letters are replete with lists of groups of people he "discipled".

  In truth, only about fifteen to twenty percent of the people you train will become trainers themselves. Don't be discouraged about this fact. Even with this percentage, God will bring about a disciple-making movement if we are faithful to broadly cast the Gospel seed.

- *They Do Training in a Non-Reproducible Way:* The key to a disciple-making movement is reproducibility. As a result, the most important people you are training are not even in the room; they are the third, fourth, and fifth generations of disciples training other disciples.

  A guiding question must be "will disciples in the following generations be able to copy exactly what I am doing and pass it to others?" What would happen if the fourth generation of believers shared, presented, facilitated, and brought the same materials to their sessions that you are? If they can follow you easily, it is reproducible. If they would have to adapt, it is non-reproducible.

9. What should I do if there are no believers in my unreached people group (UPG)?

Learn the FJT material and begin discipling and witnessing to those in your UPG. Follow Jesus Training gives seekers a good picture of who Jesus is and what it means to be a Christian. In Southeast Asia, we often disciple people and then evangelize them. FJT gives you a non-threatening way to do this.

- Locate believers in a closely connected people group–a group that has economic, political, geographic, and cultural similarities with the group you are trying to reach. Train them with the FJT material, casting a vision for reaching their friends in the adjoining people group.
- Visit Seminaries and Bible Schools to identify people from your UPG.
- Often God has already developed leaders (we are just not aware of them). Locate those who have one parent from your UPG. Many times these leaders have a burden for the UPG, but little experience in how to reach them.

10. What are the first steps for new disciples as they begin to train new disciples?

Encourage learners to follow the Simple Worship format they have practiced. The group praises together and then prays together. In the "Study" section, they teach each other one of the lessons from FJT or tell a Bible story with three application questions.

In the "Practice" section, they teach the lesson to one another again. Learners practice the Simple Worship format nine times during the seminar and have the confidence to start a disciple group when they leave.

11. What are some different venues that trainers have used these materials?

Trainers have used FJT successfully in the following ways:

- *Seminar Setting*—The best number to train in a seminar setting is 24-30 learners. The seminar lasts from two and a half to three days, depending on the educational level of the learners.

- *Weekly Sessions*—The best number to train in a weekly setting is 10-12 learners. Additional practice times for Simple Worship make the training cycle 12 weeks. Typically, the sessions are in someone's home or in a church. Some trainers lead bi-weekly groups with the understanding that the ones they are training will train others on the off week. This approach has been found to exponentially accelerate a church-planting movement.

- *Sunday School Classes*—The best number to train in a Sunday School setting is 8 to 12 learners. Because of the length of the training process, the "Study" portion of each lesson is usually split in half and taught over two Sundays. Simple Worship can be an emphasis each time, so the training lasts 20 weeks.

- *Seminary or Bible College Classes*—Trainers have used FJT in a one-week intensive equipping time and/or on a weekly basis during evangelism or discipleship classes.

- *Conferences*—Large Groups of up to one hundred learners can be trained in FJT Basic Discipleship if additional apprentices help the lead trainer with groups and with crowd logistics.

- *Sermons*—After completing FJT, pastors often teach their church the lessons. This builds interest and momentum for those who are training others to follow Jesus. The temptation, however, is to "teach" the FJT material and not "train" people with it. Pastors must guard against this danger when they use the lessons in sermons. Pastors should use the lessons as a way to empower trainers to train others in the congregation.

- *Missionary Talks*–Missionaries can share with their supporters how they train nationals in a practical way. Supporters often remark how excited they are to learn how to follow Jesus in a simple way and how the missionary is doing work on the field.

- *Coaching*–Some trainers use parts of the lessons to coach leaders in teachable moments. Since FJT is holistic (every part amplifies and explains other parts), a trainer can start at any point in the training and be assured they are giving the full picture of following Christ.

12. What should I do if non-literate or semi-literate people attend the training sessions?

Ah, the stories we could share about this subject! One will have to do. We remember well a training event in Thailand that was composed mainly of women from the northern hill tribes. In their culture, women are prohibited form learning how to read or write until they become a teenager. Of course, this means most never learn.

Usually in a training setting, the women would sit quietly and listen while the men learned. However, with the hands-on approach of Follow Jesus Training, all of the women participated in the training over a three-day period. We asked one reader to read the Scriptures aloud (instead of the entire group reading aloud together) and divided the women into groups of five or six (instead of pairs) for the training time. Tears flowed freely many times those three days as the women said, "Now we have learned something that we can give to others."

Appendix C

CHECKLISTS

Before the Training...

- *Enlist a Prayer Team*–Enlist a prayer team of twelve people to intercede for the training, before and during the training week. This is VERY important!
- *Enlist an Apprentice*–Enlist an apprentice to team-teach with you, someone who has previously attended FJT: Basic Discipleship Training.
- *Invite Participants*–Invite participants in a culturally sensitive way. This might include sending out letters, invitations, etc. The best size for FJT: Basic Discipleship Training is a seminar setting of 24-30 learners. If you have several apprentices helping you, you can train up to 100 learners. FJT: Basic Discipleship Training can also be done effectively on a weekly basis with a group of three or more learners.
- *Confirm Logistics*–Arrange housing, meals, and transportation for learners as needed.
- *Secure a Meeting Place*–Arrange a meeting room with two tables for supplies in the back of the room, chairs arranged in a circle for learners and plenty of room for learning activities during the training. If it is more appropriate,

arrange for a mat on the floor instead of chairs. Plan to provide two break times every day with coffee, tea, and snacks.

- *Collect Training Materials*–Collect Bibles, white board/ butcher paper and markers, student notes, leader notes, white poster paper for each learner for the ACTS 29 Map exercise, colored markers or crayons, notebooks (like the ones students use in school), pens, and pencils.

- *Arrange Worship Times*–Use song sheets or a chorus book for each participant. Find a person in the group who plays guitar and ask him/her to help you (if possible). The title of each lesson suggests the topic for song selection in that session.

- *Collect Active Learning Props*–Collect a balloon, a water bottle, and contest prizes.

During the Training...

- *Be Flexible*–Keep the schedule, but be flexible enough to join God in what He is doing in the lives of the learners.

- *Stress Practice and Accountability*–Make sure learners practice teaching each other the lesson after you teach them! Without practice, learners will not have the confidence to train others. It is better to shorten the lesson than to cut out the practice time. Practice and accountability are the keys to multiplication.

- *Involve Everyone in Leadership*–Ask a different person to pray at the end of each session. By the end of the training, everyone should have closed in prayer at least one time. Learners should take turns leading one part of Simple Worship in their small group time.

- *Empower and Recognize Each Learner's Gifts*–Empower participants to use their gifts during the training. Enlist learners to use their talents during the seminar: music, hospitality, prayer, teaching, humor, service, etc.

- *Review, Review, Review*—Do not skip the review section at the beginning of each session. By the end of the seminar, each learner should be able to reproduce all of the questions, answers, and hand motions. Remind learners to train each other the way you trained them. They should do the review section with the person they train each time, as well.

- *Prepare for Evaluation*—Take notes during each session about aspects of the training that learners do not understand or questions they may ask you. These notes will help you and your apprentice in the evaluation time afterwards.

- *Do Not Skip the Simple Worship Times*—Simple Worship is an integral part of the training process. As learners feel comfortable leading a Simple Worship time, they will gain confidence to begin a group after the training.

After the Training...

- *Evaluate Every Aspect of the Training with Your Apprentice*—Spend time reviewing and evaluating the training time with your apprentice. Create a list of positives and negatives. Make plans to improve the training next time you teach it.

- *Connect with Potential Apprentices about Helping In Future Trainings*—Contact two or three learners who have demonstrated leadership potential during the training about helping you with FJT: Basic Discipleship Training in the future.

- *Encourage Training Participants to Bring a Friend to the Next Training*—Encourage training participants to return with partners the next time they attend. This is an effective way of accelerating the number of trainers training others.

SCHEDULE

Use this manual to facilitate a three-day seminar or 12-week training program. Each session in both schedules takes about one and a half hours and utilizes the Training Trainers Process on page 9.

Basic Discipleship Training–Three Days

Day 1		Day 2		Day 3	
8:30	Welcome	8:30	Simple Worship	8:30	Simple Worship
10:00	Break	9:00	Obey	9:00	Share
10:15	Multiply	10:30	Break	Practice giving testimony	
12:00	Lunch	10:45	Walk	10:30	Break
1:00	Love	12:00	Lunch	10:45	Follow
3:15	Break	1:00	Simple Worship	12:00	Lunch
3:30	Pray	1:30	Go	1:00	Take-Up
5:00	Dinner	3:15	Break		
		3:30	Share		
		5:00	Dinner		

Basic Discipleship Training–Weekly

Week 1	Welcome	Week 7	Walk
Week 2	Multiply	Week 8	Simple Worship
Week 3	Love	Week 9	Go
Week 4	Simply Worship	Week 10	Share
Week 5	Pray	Week 11	Follow
Week 6	Obey	Week 12	Take Up

More Resources

Website

Current Translations

Student Books

Made in the USA
San Bernardino, CA
09 June 2016